GOD IS A PERSON

DISCOVERING GOD FOR YOURSELF
EDUCATION EDITION

PAUL D. NIXON AND CLARISE NIXON

www.TrueVinePublishing.org

God is a Person: Discovering God for Yourself
Education Edition
Paul D. Nixon and Clarise Nixon

Published by True Vine Publishing Co.
P.O. Box 22448
Nashville, TN 37202

ISBN:
978-1-956469-44-8 Paperback
978-1-956469-45-5 eBook

Copyright © 2022 by Paul D. Nixon and Clarise Nixon
All rights reserved. No part of this book may be reproduced or transmitted in any form or by any means, electronic or mechanical—including photocopying, recording, or by information storage and retrieval system—without permission in writing from the publisher.

Scriptures taken from the Holy Bible, New International Version ®, NIV®, Copyright © 1973, 1978, 1984, 2011 by Biblica, Inc ™ Used by permission of Zondervan. All rights reserved worldwide. www.zonderan.com The "NIV" and "New International Version" are trademarks registered in the United States Patent and Trademark Office by Biblica, Inc. ™

Scripture quotations are from the ESV® Bible (The Holy Bible, English Standard Version®), copyright © 2001 by Crossway Bibles, a publishing ministry of Good News Publishers. Used by permission. All rights reserved.

Scripture quotations marked NLT are taken from the Holy Bible, New Living Translation, copyright 1996, 2004, 2007, 2015 by Tyndale House Foundation. Used by permission of Tyndale House Publishers, Inc., Carol Stream, Illinois 60188

Scripture quotations marked NRSV are taken from the New Revised Standard Version Bible, copyright © 1989 National Council of the Churches of Christ in the United States of America. Used by permission. All rights reserved worldwide.

Printed in the United States of America—First Printing

To order more books, for more information about the authors, or to book for speaking engagements, go to www.cpnix.com

For Taina and Theodore with all my love.

To the Starting 5, the Boymanship Crew, Dropbox Keister, and MJKC^2:
Thank you for your support, honest feedback, laughs and love. We return the appropriate amount of positive feelings—not too much because we're introverts, but enough to satisfy your extroversion.

CONTENTS

PROLOGUE 1
INTRODUCTION 4
THE ESSENCE OF GOD 16
RIDICULOUS PRAYERS 40
CHRISTIAN ARTISTRY 65
EDEN IS A PLAYGROUND 87
SPIRITUAL DIALYSIS 104
IT'S GOD'S PREROGATIVE 126
THE PROTAGONIST PROBLEM 149
EPILOGUE 166
CRITICAL THINKING ACTIVITIES 173
STYLE QUESTIONS 175
HELPFUL RESOURCES 176

Prologue

When we were working on *God Is A Person* (*GIAP*), we couldn't help but start to think about creative ways to help students engage with the material. Even though *GIAP* is not a textbook, we think it's great content that can help students strengthen their critical thinking, reading, and writing skills. So, we decided to include resources for the classroom in this special Education Edition of the book.

Our intent is to provide questions and activities that we think will help guide you—the student— through *GIAP* so that it becomes more than just words on pages. We want the concepts to come alive for you, and we want them to be so accessible that it's rather simple to apply them in your personal lives in practical and realistic ways.

Our hope, then, is that you don't approach this as just a list of questions to get through. Our hope is that you engage with this edition as a companion text to *GIAP* so that your life is enriched in significant ways. We don't believe in "busy work" because it isn't beneficial to your learning. Thus, this edition is not intended to just be work to help you play the game of school. Instead, this edition includes resources that are intended to help guide you as you think through the material in *GIAP* and do the challenging work of putting those ideas into use in your life.

Even though each of these chapters has a set number of questions, we want you to remember that learning is never really over. Learning is a life-long activity, and it happens both in and out of classrooms, with teachers and without teachers. For these reasons, we include critical thinking activities that reference other critical thinking materials like *How to Read a Paragraph: The Art of Close Reading*, *How to Write a Paragraph: The Art of Substantive Writing*, and *The Miniature Guide to Critical Thinking Concepts & Tools*. These resources can be found at The Foundation for Critical Thinking (www.criticalthinking.org), and we strongly encourage you to read the article "College and University Students" found on their website to better understand the logic and purpose of the Pauline Tradition of critical thinking that The Foundation uses. You can find the web address to this article on the Helpful Resources page at the end of this book.

We encourage you to use this book whether your instructors assign work from it or not. We didn't create it so you could get more grades or so that your instructors could hold your hand through the material; we created it so that your own thinking and learning processes will become more autonomous and empowered.

As you use this book to build the important skills of thinking, reading, and writing, we invite you to focus your attention on God, who is the Source of all of our abilities. We pray you find this Education Edition to be a useful tool in helping you deepen your learning processes.

May God continue to bless you in your thinking as you better learn to walk with Him!

Paul and Clarise

Introduction

Learning How to See

Lunatic. Drunkard. Crazy. These are all the names John the Baptist was probably called. When people saw this man in the wilderness with his woolen hair, leather tied around his waist, pieces of locust dripping from the honey on his lips… If you've read the story, though, you would know John wasn't any of those things, but your picture is more complete than those who were around him; they didn't have the whole story like we do. But if they chose belief, John no longer looked crazy.

The fact is, John *was* a lunatic and crazy, and he *did* act like a drunkard in the eyes of some—those who didn't know or understand his purpose. And once they understood, if they chose to accept, they saw him completely differently.

Have you ever met a beautiful woman or a handsome man, and as you got to know him or her, they stopped being attractive? Or have you ever met a man or woman to whom you weren't attracted, but after spending some time together, he or she was suddenly beautiful? Their features didn't change. Their nose didn't suddenly become straighter, and their eyes didn't move closer together. Despite this, you still saw them differently because you learned he was funny and kind and intelligent; or you experienced her resilience and ingenuity and integrity. Your picture of the person became more complete, and that literally affected your eyesight.

We believe the same is true with God. The more we spend time with Him, the more we see His character and who He is, and that directly affects our attraction to Him. We get to see for ourselves not just who people say He is, but who He *really* is.

Many of us only see God through other people's words and actions, though, and we don't know Him personally. We see a mouth that says "God" and we witness the huge gap between what they say and how they live their lives, and we lose attraction to God without doing our own investigation of who God is. Not everyone who says the name of God or talks about God sees Him clearly, which means not everyone has bridged the gap between having information about God and surrendering their lives to God. Many of us get lost in the void in between information and experience, and it's really easy to drown there.

It's similar to learning how to drive. When you're a kid, you might watch intently as your parents naturally maneuver around the road and pay attention to traffic; you might intellectually understand the relationship between the clutch and the gas pedals (if they drive a stick shift), or when to start breaking if there's a stop sign or light up ahead. But when you actually get behind the wheel, all that knowledge might *help* you, but you still have to learn what it *feels like* to be behind the wheel. Knowing intellectually isn't enough; you have to have experiential knowledge to really understand the ins and outs of driving. Watching someone else drive won't teach you how to drive yourself.

It's the same in any relationship, especially a relationship with God. Observing someone else's marriage, while it can be instructive, isn't the same as being married. Someone else's friendship can give you insight into how you can be a better friend, but it isn't the same as having and *being* a friend.

You may have a good view of God right now or you might have a poor one. Whatever the case, we want to show you more of who God is so that you see Him more completely and enter into a relationship with Him for yourself.

Our Purpose

We are not trained theologians, and that is kind of the point. We believe in God, we love God, we believe the Bible is the inspired Word of God and we have dedicated our lives and careers to serving God. We are siblings and born-again Christians who work within church-sponsored organizations, but we are not professional ministers, and we also did not attend seminary. Instead, we are educators and writers who wrote this book because it is important that we acknowledge how much we *don't* yet know—about God, about other people, and even about ourselves.

Starting by acknowledging what we don't know, by being intellectually humble, is the best place for us to be; we are spiritually curious, and we hope that you are as well.

Although we are convinced that anyone may benefit from these pages, we wrote this book for those who believe in God, but don't necessarily subscribe to a particular religion; more specifically, those who have had previous religious experience and have chosen to reject organized religion for some reason.

In our conversations with others about religion, we see a common thread: many people believe God exists, but they haven't encountered a true sense of God in their previous religious experiences. Religious *culture*, then, may be a distorted lens through which the character of God is misperceived, leaving an impression of something which has religious procedure, but is not from God at all.

We believe that the negative religious experiences in Christianity that many have encountered are not accurate representations of the God who is claimed by those religious groups. We denounce racism, sexism, classism, ageism; homophobia, transphobia, xenophobia; and any other "ism," "phobia," or system of marginalization that many nominal Christians—Christians in name only, but not in practice—actively support in the name of Jesus. We believe these are violently warped views of Jesus and anything He stands for.

In our experience, distorted views of Jesus Christ are not uncommon. In fact, the traditional Western image of Jesus—a white European male who upholds the American value system—is a warped view. For centuries, many have justified all manner of hatred and division in the name of Jesus Christ, when the Jesus Christ presented in the Bible is clearly a Middle Eastern man with a collectivist, not an individualistic, understanding of culture. When we talk about Jesus Christ, we are talking about the one depicted in the Bible: an unstoppable force of love and healing among all broken people in the world.

The entire mission of Jesus Christ on Earth was reconciliation, not division: reconciliation between people and God, as well as reconciliation between people and each other. At no point in His life did Jesus condone systems or practices that marginalized others. In fact, He actively spoke out against those systems and those who financed or supported those systems in any way.

Introduction

In Matthew 23, Jesus viciously chastises the religious leaders of His time, accusing them of both preventing people from entering God's Kingdom because of their many religious laws, and also failing to enter God's Kingdom themselves because of how they mistreat other people and do not practice what they preach. When people call themselves Christians but are practicing racists or actively homophobic, for example, they fall into the same category of people that Jesus spoke directly against in Matthew 23.

To be clear, we are not suggesting that the religious institutions themselves are invalid—this is not an "anti-religion" book in that sense. Instead, we are promoting the idea that true Christianity is often mishandled by human beings, even though these people might have strong religious convictions.

We often perceive God through a distorted lens, and then draw conclusions about God based on our misperceptions. Sometimes the lens is distorted by our perspective on the purpose of religion: we may see it as an equation that puts following a specific set of rules on the same level as following God. For example, we may think, "If I just keep from doing these specific things, then God and I are ok." This misperception often leads us to think that we fully understand what we *shouldn't* do, but it usually leaves us unclear about what we *should* do and, more importantly, about who God is.

Sometimes the lens is distorted by our preferences as informed by our egocentric and sociocentric thinking. We can sometimes clearly prescribe how we would like God to operate in our favor (egocentric thinking) and in the favor of those who are part of our immediate society or culture (sociocentric thinking). Both of these types of thinking create a "me/us vs.

them" dynamic, which is a distortion of the image of God and not part of His original plan for humanity. We have difficulty when we perceive God as acting for or in the favor of people and groups who we view as opposing us.

Sometimes the lens is distorted by a misunderstanding of how we relate to God, or rather, how God relates to us. We are unclear about what we should receive from God and what we should give to Him, or whether we should be standing over God, under Him, or next to Him.[1]

And sometimes this lens is distorted by good ol' "church folk." We hear what they say and then we see what they are like, and we either accept or reject the image of God they are giving us with the misunderstanding that those people are the full, accurate image of God. We either like or don't like them, so we make a decision about God based on the people who claim to represent Him. But it is important that we realize no person, except for Jesus Christ Himself, is a completely accurate representation of God.

In his book *Immeasurable: Reflections on the Soul of Ministry in the Age of Church, Inc.*, Skye Jethani writes about the idea of Proximity vs. Platform. He essentially asks, what is the reason we are giving people or organizations authority in our lives? Is it that they are popular and thus have a strong platform; or is it that we are close to them and thus have the proximity we need to evaluate the truth of what they claim?

As it relates to church, we often accept or reject church based on platform, not based on proximity. We either like or dislike the pastor, the music, the style of worship, the kind of

---

[1] Jethani, Skye. *With: Reimagining the Way You Relate to God.* Thomas Nelson Publishers, 2011.

Introduction

outreach the church does, the fact that our family goes there, or some other external factor, and we make a decision about God based on the church's platform. But when it comes to the day-to-day operations of our lives, we don't give God the authority He deserves because we do not have any real proximity to Him; we haven't actually built a relationship with Him.

Anything except a genuine, close relationship with God and with His people will be easy to abandon when something related to the platform goes wrong. The Apostle Paul says it this way in Philippians 3:7-11 (NLT):

> I once thought these things [following various religious rules] were valuable, but now I consider them worthless because of what Christ has done. Yes, everything else is worthless when compared with the infinite value of knowing Christ Jesus my Lord. For his sake I have discarded everything else, counting it all as garbage, so that I could gain Christ and become one with him. I no longer count on my own righteousness through obeying the law; rather, I become righteous through faith in Christ. For God's way of making us right with himself depends on faith. I want to know Christ and experience the mighty power that raised him from the dead. I want to suffer with him, sharing in his death, so that one way or another I will experience the resurrection from the dead!

Paul considered knowing God as a person through the death and resurrection of Jesus Christ to be the most valuable thing in his life. We agree with him.

While we do not systematically disassemble each of the possible misperceptions about God, we do make an effort to avoid them in our presentation. In these pages, we attempt to re-imagine God how He really is while trying not to lean into any religious system. Again, we are not taking an anti-religion stance in this book. In fact, we ourselves are in favor of religion when it is utilized properly (i.e. fully and centrally bound by the love of God). We ourselves are active, practicing Christians. But we believe that, for the Christian, religion is a means to an end, not the end in itself.

We think of religions like vehicles: there are coupes, SUVs and even pickup trucks. The vehicles are all going to the same destination, though not at the same pace or through the same twists and turns. We believe that any of these vehicles, *when driven by God*, will follow the right path and make it to the desired destination through Jesus Christ: eternal life in Heaven with Him. When God is driving, He is in charge of the car, the path, the speed, and the overall journey. The problem with many religions is that they are typically driven by fallible humans, not perfect God. The idea that "God is my co-pilot" is a perfect example of the kind of thinking that gets religious people and religious systems off track. God shouldn't be 2nd in command; He should be 1st.

We want to represent who God really is and make it clear that the path to Him is through Jesus Christ. The journey to God won't be the same for every person, but Jesus Christ is the bridge between God and humanity, and Jesus is not bound by (i.e. limited to) anything, including religion, because God is a divine Person.

Introduction

We believe in fairmindedness, and therefore, it is critical that we consider some other perspectives of the things we know so little about. We believe the Holy Bible is God's word, and that God uses it to communicate with people even today. The Bible teaches that God's methods differ greatly from man's methods, and that God's ideals and standards are significantly higher than ours.[2] Couple this truth with the understanding that we as humans already don't know so much, and you may better understand our motivation for writing this book.

By no means do we think that we as the writers of this book have all the correct answers, or that our ideas are somehow higher or better than another person's. While we have been members of the Christian church our entire lives, the concepts we present in this book are somewhat unique to our experience. We came to these conclusions outside of the religious structure to which we belong. Simply put, the Holy Spirit impressed us with some ideas, we wrote them down, and then put them together in the form of the book that you are now reading.

There are innumerable truths about God—about His essence, His nature, His love for humanity, the way He chooses to deal with us—that we have yet to apprehend. So, we present these ideas as slivers of truth from admittedly flawed (but still Christ-led) perspectives with the prayerful hope that they may help you come a little closer to understanding who God really is. In these pages, we reimagine God and present Him without any man-made constructs.

---

[2] Isaiah 55:8-9 (NIV): "For my thoughts are not your thoughts, neither are your ways my ways," declares the Lord. "As the heavens are higher than the earth, so are my ways higher than your ways and my thoughts than your thoughts."

Each chapter in this book is intended to stand alone as a reimagination of one aspect of an everyday, practical life with God. The chapters begin with a biblically-inspired guiding principle and they end with practical steps to help you enrich your walk with God.

We are academicians, so we're used to writing in an essay-style format. We recognize, however, that having footnotes doesn't always make for the smoothest reading experience. We decided to keep these notes in our book, though, because they point to the Bible. And because God is a person, and His story is written in the Book, it's a great place to learn more about Him. We hope the footnotes encourage you to read the Bible even if the notes slightly alter your reading experience with our material.

We hope this book sparks your imagination and your intellect. And, in all things, we pray that your walk with Jesus Christ benefits from what you read here.

We invite you to journey with us.

Introduction

COMPREHENSION QUESTIONS BASED ON THE CHAPTER

1. What is the rhetorical situation (communicator, audience, and message) of the chapter, and why does this context matter?
2. What is the stated or implied thesis statement of the introduction?
3. What lenses do the authors say might distort the image of God if we try to view God through those lenses?
4. Explain proximity vs platform.
5. Why do the authors think using footnotes could be limiting, and why did they decide to use them anyway?

Writing Questions

1. Explain the difference between observing a relationship and participating in a relationship. What are some things that you cannot learn through observation, and that you can only learn through participation?
2. Explore one of the distorted views about God that you have had in the past, or that you have seen on display, either in religious people or in non-religious people. What are some ways to ensure that your view of God is full and accurate?
3. Analyze the car metaphor on p. 11. Does this metaphor effectively capture the idea that the authors are trying to convey? If it does, explain how it is effective. If it does not, think of some ways that the metaphor could be improved to better make the point.

4. Read and annotate Matthew 23 (using the Logic Of if necessary). Golden Rule: every underline/highlight needs a corresponding comment.

The Essence of God

God is a loving Person. God's love is expressed through His "omnis," and in order to properly understand God's character, we must do so with His primary attribute as the interpretive key.

1 John 4:7-8 (NIV)
Dear friends, let us love one another, for love comes from God. Everyone who loves has been born of God and knows God. Whoever does not love does not know God, because God is love.

In March of 1971, the Ira H. Hardin Company broke ground on a new stadium in Atlanta, Georgia. Considered to be one of the great architectural marvels of its time, this stadium was going to take advantage of new structural designs and seating concepts. It cost about $17 million to build it back then—over $100 million by modern standards. The roofing design in particular was unique. It was designed with Cor-Ten weathering steel, which is covered in rust. They built the roof using rust so that when the roof continued to rust, it would become a protective seal which would form a solid steel structure that would last for a lifetime. They called it The Omni.[1]

The word "omni" is derived from Latin. In English, it normally forms a prefix which means "all." For example, an animal that eats any kind of food is called an *omni*vore, and a vehicle intended to carry all kinds of passengers is called an *omni*bus.

As a stadium, The Omni was to host all kinds of entertainment events. It was home to the Atlanta Hawks basketball team, the Atlanta Flames hockey team, and three different indoor soccer teams. It served as the primary concert venue for the city of Atlanta, hosting hundreds of concerts by big name acts including Elvis Presley, Madonna, Bruce Springsteen, Whitney Houston, Prince, and Michael Jackson. The Omni was even a hotbed for professional wrestling. Many major and historic wrestling events took place there such as Georgia Championship Wrestling, the WCW, and the WWF, now called the WWE. The Omni even held the 1988 Democratic National Convention.

Despite all its success, The Omni was misnamed. It began to look dated in the early 90s, despite being only 20 years old. The supposedly advanced seating plan with its 16 luxury boxes and no club level was being totally outclassed by newer arenas with over 200 luxury boxes and much better amenities for high end customers.

But the biggest problem was with the roof—the part of the building that was supposed to be its claim to fame. The steel of

---

[1] Fincher, James R. "Atlanta's New Coliseum." *Modern Steel Construction*, XV, no. 1, 1975, pp. 3-5

the roof was not properly designed to withstand the climate of the city of Atlanta, so it began to corrode much earlier than anticipated. First, the roof began to leak water. Later, large gaps formed, creating holes so big that fans could climb through and watch events for free! The plan to include rust in the roof to make it more secure backfired, and The Omni had to be demolished in 1997.

And a fundamental failing of humanity is revealed. As much as we know, and as much as we can do, we cannot create, nor can we be, *omni*. He is the only Omni. And studying God's "omni's" illuminates something new about His character.

In order to properly interpret God's character, we must do so with His primary attribute as the interpretive key, which is found in 1 John 4:7-8.

God is the ultimate source of other-centeredness, the perfect example of "you first, me second." This is *love*. In fact, God takes it even further than that, and in doing so, He reveals how short we come of His standard of what love truly is. For God, love is "you first, even if I am destroyed in the process." God loves fully, recklessly, self-sacrificially, and we are always the object of His love. This self-sacrificial love is illustrated perfectly with Jesus' death on the cross; He died for us *so that* we could reconnect with God.

Except for Biblical examples and in the life of Jesus Christ, nowhere else will you find someone advocating for self-sacrificing love to the degree of self-destruction. No pastor or counselor will recommend that you die for someone, especially someone who is actively mistreating you. But that is exactly what Jesus did for us, because that is just the kind of person that God is.

And this is why self-sacrificial love, God's love, is so counter-cultural, because we don't see it in our culture to the degree that Jesus illustrated it. Because humanity and our culture fall short of God's standard of love, it is only possible through His supernatural power. We need His help to even wrap our minds around the idea that self-sacrificial love is healthy because it sounds very destructive and unhealthy. And it actually is, without God. We wouldn't recommend self-sacrificial love apart from God.

According to the Bible, not only does love come from God, but love is God. God does not merely *generate* love, God *is* love, and God is a person. It is impossible for love to be healthily and fully developed apart from God, including self-love.

The popular definition of self-love in Western culture is "me first *so that* I can love others." This definition has been immortalized, among other places, in the song "Greatest Love of All," popularized by Whitney Houston in 1986. Houston sings, "Learning to love yourself, it is the greatest love of all." This definition of self-love, however, omits the most important aspect of love; namely, our identity in Christ. Therefore, this definition falls short of what the fullest sense of love really means. True love must be revealed through the One who *is* love: God.[2] When we begin anywhere else, we're bound to distort love somehow and somewhere.

We are not arguing that we should ignore our needs in favor of the needs of others. In fact, we believe that a person who does not take care of themselves—spiritually, emotionally,

---

[2] John 17:26 (NLT): "...I have revealed you to them, and I will continue to do so. Then your love for me will be in them, and I will be in them."

physically, etc.—will not bring their healthiest selves to a love relationship. During Jesus' ministry on Earth, He often went to a secluded place to get away from the crowds and rest.

You are the temple of God[3] and you are made in His image.[4] How you treat yourself, then, matters and affects you in very significant ways; it's a larger representation of who God is. We wholeheartedly believe in self-care, but self-care is about more than lighting candles and taking baths and giving yourself a spa night. You should also pay attention to your self-talk; evaluate the people you've let into your life and how they treat you, listen to you, speak to you: do you speak to God in those same ways? Are you reverent and loving with Him? Look at the boundaries you've set up in your life: are they all healthy? What does your "healthy" even look like? Have you included spiritual time in your self-care routine?

> "How you treat yourself... matters and affects you in very significant ways"

We should address our self-care needs through Christ, the ultimate embodiment of love. In order to fully understand love and therefore practice true love, we need to build a relationship with God so He can teach us what true love even means, whether that love is directed toward Him, ourselves, or others.

We can *fake* love without God, as we do with things such as lust, obsession, infatuation, codependency and more. These

---

[3] 1 Cor. 3:16-17 (NLT): "Don't you realize that all of you together are the temple of God and that the Spirit of God lives in you? God will destroy anyone who destroys this temple. For God's temple is holy, and you are that temple."
[4] Gen. 1:27 (NIV): "So God created mankind in his own image, in the image of God he created them; male and female he created them."

counterfeits may share common attributes with true love; for example, *passion* is a component of both lust and genuine love. But it is possible to feel passion without the necessary components of love. While love is "you first, me second," lust is just the opposite: lust is "me first right now, you can come along if you want."

Without God, every attempt we make at generating love will end in a sham. Every act of selflessness, every case of altruism, every instance of *true* other-centeredness finds its root in God because God is love. So, since God is love, everything He does is an act of love, and every attribute that He has is sourced by His love.

Think of God's love as a pair of glasses that has the perfect prescription. People who wear glasses rarely go a day, or even an hour, without their glasses. Because their vision is distorted, though they can see without their glasses, they cannot see clearly at all. In the same way, without our "love glasses," we will be able to see God's attributes, but we will not be able to see them clearly, thus making it easy to misunderstand God. Considering God through the lens of love turns our old VHS tape in standard definition into an Ultra 4K Blu-ray with crystal clear HD.

Re-watching an old movie after it has been visually restored can be like watching a completely different film. This is how it will be when we consider God's omnis, but this time through the magnificent prism of His everlasting love.

God's Omniscience

Omniscient is a compound word that is a combination of "omni" and "science." Omni means *all* and *science* is the word for knowledge. Basically, omniscience means that God has infinite awareness, understanding and insight: God knows everything. We tend to think of science as a particular discipline of study, a specific kind of knowing. But the first definition of the word science is simply "knowledge." Some people try to put the discipline of science and God at opposite ends of the spectrum, as though we have to choose between God and science, but science is one of God's creations. Science is only fully scientific when it is viewed as a component of God's creativity. We can uncover pieces of knowledge without God, but we can never understand the fullness of science apart from God. God is omniscient, science is not.

The Limitations of Science

In 2019, theoretical physicist Marcelo Gleiser won the Templeton Prize, a yearly prize from the John Templeton Foundation given to a scientist "who has made an exceptional contribution to affirming life's spiritual dimension, whether through insight, discovery or practical works."[5] Previous recipients of the award include scientists Sir Martin Rees and Freeman Dyson, and religious leaders Mother Teresa, the Dalai Lama, and Archbishop Desmond Tutu.[6] Dr. Gleiser is a

---

[5] "Marcelo Gleiser Awarded 2019 Templeton Prize." *John Templeton Foundation,* 6 Aug. 2020, https://www.templeton.org/news/marcelo-gleiser-awarded-2019-templeton-prize

[6] Ibid.

proponent of *consilience*, the need for humility in science. He says:

> I believe we should take a much humbler approach to knowledge, in the sense that if you look carefully at the way science works, you'll see that, yes it is wonderful - magnificent! - but it has limits. And we have to understand and respect those limits. And by doing that, by understanding how science advances, science really becomes a deeply spiritual conversation with the mysterious, about all the things we don't know. [7]

Dr. Gleiser is also opposed to the idea of atheism. Here's what he says on the subject:

> I honestly think atheism is inconsistent with the scientific method. What I mean by that is, what is atheism? It's a statement, a categorical statement that expresses belief in non belief. "I don't believe even though I have no evidence for or against, simply I don't believe." Period. It's a declaration. But in science we don't really do declarations. [8]

Dr. Gleiser acknowledges the limitations of human knowledge and science, but because he aligns himself primarily with science, he still falls short of the mark because he has no

---
[7] Billings, Lee. "Atheism Is Inconsistent with the Scientific Method, Prizewinning Physicist Says." *Scientific American*, Scientific American, 20 Mar. 2019, www.scientificamerican.com/article/atheism-is-inconsistent-with-the-scientific-method-prizewinning-physicist-says/.
[8] Ibid.

evidence of God. Dr. Gleiser truly reveals the limitation of science—it is based on evidence and observation, but we know that we cannot observe everything, and there are many things for which we will never find evidence. Dr. Gleiser considers himself an agnostic. He admits to the limits of science, but he has not yet aligned himself with He who has no limits—the omniscient God.

In fact, Dr. Gleiser proposes that science has "brought humankind back to the metaphorical center of creation—his doctrine of 'humancentrism'—by revealing the improbable uniqueness of our planet, and the exceptional rarity of humans as intelligent beings capable of understanding the importance of being alive."[9] Without God to guide our scientific discoveries, we end up minimizing God and idolizing ourselves.

The key to life on this earth is not the acquisition of scientific evidence that we can verify, but faith in the One who is beyond our ability to verify. As followers of God, faith is all the evidence we need.

This is illustrated in the fact that many things take place in the world that our science cannot explain. In his book *Redemption in Genesis: The Crossroads of Faith and Reason*, Dr. John Nixon, Sr. says:

> As believers, we don't limit ourselves to just two options, as if we have to choose either the rational or the irrational. Rather, we acknowledge the existence of another category peculiar to the spiritual realm, that of

---

[9] "Marcelo Gleiser Awarded 2019 Templeton Prize." *John Templeton Foundation*, 6 Aug. 2020, https://www.templeton.org/news/marcelo-gleiser-awarded-2019-templeton-prize

the superrational. The existence of a superrational reality means that there are truths that fall into a category that isn't logical but isn't illogical either. There are truths that possess the characteristics of logic—they are sensible, clear, and based on sound reasoning—yet that break through the boundaries of what is quantifiable and explainable. They reach beyond the limits of logic.[10]

For the believer, both science and logic fall short of the superrational. The Bible is God's own text of the *superrational.*

Applying Superrational Thinking

The Bible testifies to God's omniscience. Psalm 147:4-5 (NIV) says, "He determines the number of the stars and calls them each by name. Great is our Lord and mighty in power; His understanding has no limit." 1 John 3:20b (ESV) says, "God is greater than our heart, and he knows everything." The Bible says that, not only does God *know* the truth, God *is* the truth. God generates truth, so what God says is real.

God's word is creative. That is to say, if God says something, it becomes true because He said it. Just look at the creation story in Genesis.[11] God says, let there be, and there just is. For example, God created light on the first day,[12] and didn't create the sun until the fourth day,[13] so what was illuminating everything on days two, three, and four? We think of the sun as Earth's source of light, but the sun is merely the governor. The

---

[10] Nixon, John. *Redemption in Genesis: the Crossroads of Faith and Reason.* Pacific Press Pub. Association, 2011, pp. 13-14
[11] Genesis ch. 1
[12] Genesis 1:3 (NIV): "And God said, 'Let there be light,' and there was light."
[13] Genesis 1:14-19

sun doesn't create light, God does. What God says *is*, and it is part of the nature of His omniscience.

But if we're honest, there is something off-putting about this concept. We prefer to be *not* known, because being known makes us feel vulnerable. Look at how Hebrews 4:13 puts it in the ESV: "And no creature is hidden from his sight, but all are naked and exposed to the eyes of Him to Whom we must give account." Why do I have to be naked and exposed? And it sounds like I have to have a report ready too. Am I naked when I give the report? This sounds like a very uncomfortable situation.

Look at Psalm 139 (ESV): "O Lord, you have searched me and know me! You know when I sit down and when I rise up; you discern my thoughts from afar. You search out my path and my lying down and are acquainted with all my ways. Even before a word is on my tongue, behold, O Lord, you know it altogether." Does it sound a little limiting? Is God being restrictive here?

Verse 5 says, "You hem me in, behind and before, and lay your hand upon me." It might seem like it, but God is not confining us in this text; that's what the devil would have us believe. It's the same lie he told Eve in the Garden of Eden. God framed Adam and Eve's existence as great freedom with an infinitesimal restriction, and even that restriction was to save their lives. Satan came in the form of a serpent and re-framed it as great restriction for the sake of God's own selfish purposes (*see* "Ridiculous Prayers"). It was an effective deception because, as we know, Eve ate the forbidden fruit and gave it to Adam, who ate as well.[14] And humanity is still falling for the same lie to this day: if we obey God, we will not be able to do what we want or have any fun (*see* "Eden Is a Playground").

Psalm 139:3 in the ASV says, "You scrutinize my path and my lying down, and are intimately acquainted with all my ways." *Scrutinize* is a verb meaning, "to examine closely and minutely." The dictionary defines it this way: "to examine in detail with careful or critical attention." Without considering this verse as being within the realm of God's love, a person might misunderstand what the text is saying and misunderstand God's intent.

Growing up, whenever we would go out to eat with our family, our father would always scrutinize the bill before he paid it. Perhaps others do something similar. It's possible that people scrutinize their receipt when they leave the grocery store. Or maybe they scrutinize the cashier to make sure he rings it up correctly in the first place. The word *scrutinize* can have a negative connotation when we apply it to a person. When God applies it to us, it has a different purpose.

We can see how it's possible for some people to be turned off from the Bible, how the word of God can be unattractive to someone who approaches it in a particular way. If we aren't careful, we can misrepresent God as being intrusive and selfish when in fact He is the opposite of those things, because neither of those things are loving attributes. God does not seek intrusion, He seeks intimacy; He is not selfish, taking things for Himself, He is selfless, giving everything of Himself; He is not trying to restrict us, He is trying to set us free.

---

[14] Genesis ch. 3

The Essence of God

Without our love glasses on, it could seem like God's omniscience is not working in our favor. But it is, however, because God's omniscience is a component of His love.

We tend to think of God's omniscience in terms of information, and it is true that God has all information. But if God is wielding omniscience so He can love us better, we would be better off thinking of God's omniscience in terms of preparation. God uses His omniscience to love us by making a path for us. God is ready for every possible eventuality, and He has made a way of escape out of every mistake we haven't even made yet. God understands our character and our broken nature. He not only knows that we will make mistakes, He knows every mistake we could possibly make, and He has made a way out for each and every one of them.[15] And because God's word is creative, He can create an escape when there is none.

And He doesn't only make a way out when we get into trouble; He makes a way in, giving us opportunities to succeed when there would otherwise have been no hope.

Loving Omniscience in Action

God answering a prayer before it is even prayed is an example of God's loving omniscience on full display (*see* "Ridiculous Prayers"). When our dad was 11, he was hit by a car. He was not seriously injured, and life continued. Fast forward 10 years to the mid-1970s, and our dad wanted to marry his girlfriend. So, they were preparing to get married, and

---

[15] 1 Cor. 10:13 (NLT): "The temptations in your life are no different from what others experience. And God is faithful. He will not allow the temptation to be more than you can stand. When you are tempted, he will show you a way out so that you can endure."

our dad prayed to God asking for a sign. He asked God to send him some money if He wanted them to get married. This was not a prayer of greed, but a prayer of necessity. Our dad wasn't trying to buy a new stereo or a new pair of sneakers. He was only trying to get a place to live so he could be a husband.

He was living in the college dorm at the time. One day, the phone in the dorm hall rang. He picked up the phone and it was his mother, our grandmother, on the line. She said, "Johnny, do you remember when you were hit by that car when you were 11?" Dad said, "Yes, I remember." Grandma said, "The city of New York has written you a check for damages from that accident."

This was not a case of mere coincidence. Grandma told our dad that it took so long for the case to be resolved because every time the case made it to the top of a judge's pile, something would happen to transfer the case to another judge, and it would go back to the bottom of the pile. The first judge retired, the second judge passed away, the third judge moved to another state. Over and over again, judges had changes of circumstance so the case was delayed and delayed for many years until finally, at the precise time when our dad needed money so he could marry our mom, our grandmother was holding a check for him. Our family is a living example of God's loving omniscience on full display. So now, like Joseph, everyone in our family can say that what may have been meant for evil (dad getting hit by a car), God used for good.

God uses His loving omniscience (i.e. His information) to help us with our problems and reveal His character to us.

To Infinity…

God is infinite. The infinite is one of God's omnis, and it includes two concepts: space and time. God has no limits in either of these areas. Another form of the word *infinity* is *infinitude*. The word for God's infinitude in space is *omnipresence* and the word for God's infinitude in time is *eternity*.

Omnipresence

God is omnipresent. This means that God is everywhere all the time. He is not present *in* everything, He is present *to* everything. And He isn't here or there in part; He's everywhere in full.

The fullness of God's character is always present.[16][17][18]

The Bible makes it clear that God is omnipresent. God is here and he is there. God is in Turkey and He is in China. God is in Ethiopia and He is in Brazil. He's everywhere, and He isn't only in the places that He thinks you should be. When we were younger, we sometimes heard older Christians say, "If you go into the club, your angels stay outside." But the Bible does not support that thinking. Psalm 139:8 in the KJV says it differently: *"if I make my bed in hell*, behold, thou art there" (emphasis added). Even if we choose to live outside God's will for us, He still doesn't leave us.

---

[16] Colossians 1:17 (ESV) - "And he is before all things, and in him all things hold together."

[17] Jeremiah 23:24 (NRSV) - "Who can hide in secret places so that I cannot see them? says the Lord. Do I not fill heaven and earth? says the Lord."

[18] Psalm 139:8-10 (NIV) - "If I go up to the heavens, you are there; if I make my bed in the depths, you are there. If I rise on the wings of the dawn, if I settle on the far side of the sea, even there your hand will guide me, your right hand will hold me fast."

Eternity

God is everywhere, not only in terms of place, but also in terms of time. Time is a creation, and God is not subject to any of His creations. God operates on His creation, not the other way around. God does not experience life in a linear fashion, the way humans do. God is not inside the timeline, waiting for one thing to happen before He can do the next thing. Instead, because God is eternal, He always has been and always will be.

Without our love glasses on, this might seem like a negative attribute. Proverbs 15:3 (ESV) says, "The eyes of the Lord are in every place, keeping watch on the evil and the good." That could sound like spying, which is very uncomfortable. If we're not careful, we can reduce God to a voyeuristic neighbor with a pair of cosmic binoculars. This can be our thinking when we fail to categorize God's infinitude as an attribute of His love. This can also be uncomfortable for us emotionally because God can see our "dark places," the areas we don't even want to look at ourselves.

God's Loving Infinitude

God isn't watching us for no reason. God uses His infinitude to love us better. We might think that God is merely spying on us, but it is better to think of God's infinitude in terms of attention: we have God's full attention all the time. God is completely present to all of our moments, which is very different from our interactions with other people. Sometimes at the end of a long day, you might be listening to your spouse or friend, and you're having a hard time paying attention because you're so tired or distracted. One of you thinks you are having a good conversation, and the next thing you know the other one is asleep. This happens because we do not have unlimited attention. But God does. God's infinitude means He has unlimited attention, and He spends all of it on each of us all the time.

It's becoming less and less realistic for a person to expect to be able to have someone else's undivided attention for an extended period of time. There is so much going on, and we give our full attention to so few things. But God's attention never wavers.

James 5:13 and 14 (ESV) says, "Is anyone among you suffering? Let him pray. Is anyone cheerful? Let him sing praise. Is anyone among you sick? Let him call for the elders of the church, and let them pray over him, anointing him with oil in the name of the Lord." Prayer is a conversation with God, and He wants to talk to us all the time, no matter what we have going on in our lives. God's omnipresence means He is always ready for us to come to Him, He is always waiting to hear from us, and we have His full attention all of the time.

God's Omnipotence

Maybe the most fun omni to imagine is God's omnipotence, which means God has all power and all ability. In this age of superhero shows and movies, it's fun to think of God flying around, deflecting bullets, walking through walls. Without our love glasses, it can be very easy to reduce God to a comic book character, but comic book characters are flawed, so thinking of God in this way distorts who He is.

Not only is God's omnipotence fun to imagine, it can also be confusing. Not because we don't believe it to be true, but because we *do* believe it to be true. God's omnipotence is the attribute that people most readily accept of God. The most common and the most easily accepted image of God is an image of power.

This is the case for the true God, and for the fictional gods as well. Imagine Wonder Woman, the mighty Amazon flying through the air to save the day. Conjure an image of Black Panther, the powerful Wakandan warrior, leading his troops to victory in glorious battle. When we think of supernatural beings, we think of them first as beings of power. This is an appropriate image for such beings. Indeed, if our superheroes weren't stronger and faster than us, then they wouldn't deserve to be our superheroes. We want our heroes, our superheroes, and our gods to be gods of power, because that is what we want for ourselves. We make our heroes in our image, possessing the things that we wish we had, so that when we dream, we can dream of being them.

God, the true God, is the God of supreme, ultimate power. But He is not made in our image. We are made in His image. We make the mistake of assuming that, because God is all-powerful, it means that He should use His power the way *we* would use it if *we* were all-powerful. When He doesn't use His power in this way, we sometimes call Him corrupt or even evil. When we witness atrocities every day in our world and in our personal lives, we conclude that God cannot be all good and all-powerful at the same time. We use the scientific method, instead of the superrational method, when we observe then report.

If God is both good and powerful, then why does He let small children endure abuse? If God is both good and powerful, then why does He allow women to be beaten by their husbands? If God is both good and powerful, then why is there so much social injustice in the world? It seems like God either doesn't care about all this suffering, or He can't stop it.

The problem with this image of God is that it is inherently selfish. It's not really about God, it's about us. We have this picture of a God who will beat up all of our enemies, who will repay the bullies who treated us bad when we were in high school, who will make fools of the people who made fun of us. God will fight our battles, and He will destroy sin, but He will do it using His own methods and in His own time.

God Fights His Own Way

1 Kings 18 tells the story of the prophet Elijah challenging 450 prophets of the god Baal to a "whose God is real" contest. Elijah had 2 altars made, one for him and one for them, and had a bull laid on each one, but neither

> "This is how we imagine the power of God: humiliating our enemies and getting vengeance for us."

offering was set on fire. The contest was that both groups would call to their God, and the real God would answer and send fire to the altar. Baal's prophets went first. The Bible says they called upon the name of Baal from morning until noon. In verse 27 (NLT), Elijah started talking trash when he said, "You'll have to shout louder… for surely he is a god! Perhaps he is daydreaming, or is relieving himself. Or maybe he is away on a trip, or is asleep and needs to be wakened!" The Bible says the prophets of Baal cut themselves and shouted louder, but nobody answered.

Then Elijah made a big display of digging a trench around his altar and pouring buckets of water on it 3 times, enough to fill the trench. Then he prayed to God, and verse 38 (NLT) says: "Immediately the fire of the Lord flashed down from heaven and burned up the young bull, the wood, the stones, and the dust. It even licked up all the water in the trench!"

This is how we imagine the power of God: humiliating our enemies and getting vengeance for us. And we imagine ourselves in Elijah's position, mocking the naysayers and basking in the glory of victory. But in this story, God didn't win the victory for Elijah, God used Elijah to win the victory for Himself. It was God's glory, not Elijah's, because God was the one with the power. Elijah was just a messenger, a vessel for God's glory to shine through. Our image of God's power often has us on the receiving end of applause because we think of ourselves as the central figure in the story, not God (*see* "The Protagonist Problem").

We think of God as simply having more of the same kind of power than our enemy does. The enemy has power, but God has more of it, so God wins. But if we think about the life of Jesus on Earth, we will notice that Jesus did not use the same kind of power that Satan was using. Jesus did not use the power of domination; He used the power of submission. His power was not in taking, but in giving; not in hitting, but in being hit; not in taking life, but in laying down His life. Jesus ruled through service because the Kingdom of God is a Kingdom of love, which means those in God's Kingdom are *other-centered*. They are not focused on what they can get; they are instead focused on what they can give. Jesus demonstrated that God rules with a totally different kind of power than the devil even has access to.

Reframing God's Omnis

So, with this in mind, let's consider the other side of the coin of God's omnipotence. Let's not think of omnipotence in terms of strength, but let's think of omnipotence in terms of stamina, specifically, emotional energy. God has an endless supply of emotional energy, which means He never gets tired of hearing our cares and bearing our burdens. He will never cease to be able to carry our load, not with us, but for us.

Jesus says, "Step aside, I'll take it. Lay it on me, I'll carry it."[19] God uses His omnipotence to love us by making His infinite stamina available to us. He wields His unlimited strength, not just to smite down His enemies, but to uphold His children and to carry our burdens for us.

Picture God how He really is. Not controlling, nosy, and harsh, but giving, intimate, and gentle. God is omniscient, He is omnipresent, and He is omnipotent, but all of those things take a back seat to God's ultimate omni: God is all love, which means that all of God's attributes must be centered around His love. Because all of His attributes are centered around His love, it takes the superrational to understand how God's surrender and sacrifice for sinful humanity led to victory over evil and sin.

All acts of true love find their source in God, as God is the one source of all pure other-centeredness in the entire Universe.

---

[19] Psalm 55:22; Isaiah 46:4; Isaiah 40:10; Matthew 11:28-30

Practical Steps for Discovering the Essence of God

1. Think of God as a person with feelings

   - Build a relationship with God the way you would build a relationship with a person. What types of conversations do you have with your friends? What kinds of plans do you make with one another? What kinds of jokes do you tell? What do you share?

   - Don't only focus on what you're getting out of the relationship, but pay attention to what you're giving to the relationship.

2. Think of prayer as a time to listen and learn, not just to speak. Ask God to lay things on your heart that He wants to talk to you about that day.

3. Ask relationship-building questions of God

   - How are You feeling?

   - How can I support Your kingdom and ultimate plan today?

   - What's my role in my relationship with You?

   - Do you want me to listen right now or respond?

COMPREHENSION QUESTIONS BASED ON THE CHAPTER

1. What is the rhetorical situation (communicator, audience, and message) of the chapter, and why does this context matter?
2. What is the stated or implied thesis statement of the chapter?
3. What is one main difference between God's love and human love?
4. How can self-love be *other*-centered?
5. Briefly describe what *love glasses* do. What are some consequences of *not* using love glasses?
6. What is *superrational* thinking?

Writing Questions
1. Think of a time in your life or in the life of someone you know when God's loving omniscience was on display. Briefly tell the story and write a reflection on God's love in that situation.
2. Explain how it's possible that God not only *knows* truth, but He *is* truth.
3. Explore the ways in which having God's full attention all the time can be to your benefit. Why is it important to remember that God is always paying attention to you, not as a spy, but as a loving friend and a concerned parent?
4. Compare and contrast God with your favorite comic book character or superhero. How is God's power different from the character's power?

5. Read and annotate 1 Kings 18 (using the Logic Of if necessary). Golden Rule: every underline/highlight needs a corresponding comment.

Ridiculous Prayers

God is a freeing Person. If we have an idea, no matter how ridiculous, God can match and surpass it.

Ephesians 3:20 (NIV)
Now to him who is able to do immeasurably more than all we ask or imagine, according to his power that is at work within us...

We have a brother named John who is a minister. He sometimes shares a sermon illustration that demonstrates the freedom we can have within certain boundaries. When his children were young, they used to like playing in the front yard. Because of the danger and proximity to the road, though, John found himself constantly on edge and telling them to be careful every two minutes, which took away some of the joy of the kids being outside in the first place. When they played in the backyard within the boundary of the fence that surrounded the area, though, John didn't have to worry about them being hit by oncoming traffic, so the kids experienced much more freedom and joy because they were in a safe, enclosed space.

In the front yard, the kids were *too free*, which required them to need constant supervision, direction, and re-direction. But within the boundaries of the fenced-in backyard, the kids were totally safe, so they could play without much supervision at all.

In the backyard, they could do whatever they wanted, but while in the front yard they had to be extra cautious.

The idea, then, is that boundaries aren't constricting, at least not when they are an expression of love. Boundaries actually make us more free (*see* "Eden is a Playground").

This example highlights an important misunderstanding of what freedom really means, or what it *can* mean. We take "freedom" to mean that we can do whatever we want without restriction. The problem is, we don't always consider the implications of where our limited and often sinful desires can lead us. As a result, we find ourselves "too free" when we operate without any boundaries. It's like we're in the front yard where there are dangerous cars, stray animals and strangers from whom we need constant protection. We end up going places that are not actually better for us and being with people with whom we think we will enjoy ourselves, but who actually hurt us.

> "...boundaries aren't constricting, at least not when they are an expression of love."

Spiritual freedom, which we call *full freedom*, is sweeter and more gratifying than the oversimplified idea of *partial freedom* which begins and ends with "I want to do this, so I will." Full freedom is the ability to be who we were created to be by God. When we surrender our will to God, we find limitless potential and ability. Within God's loving boundaries, we are able to do anything we want because what we want is in line with what

God wants for us.[1] It's like we're in the fenced-in backyard. Full freedom comes with no shame or guilt attached to it; instead, it leads to mental and emotional liberation. It's a more robust expression of the fulfillment we seek in partial freedom.

An Insatiable Hunger

There are so many unintended consequences to our limited understanding of freedom. Worry and stress can easily overwhelm us when we are trying to fulfill our own desires. We constantly want more, and we're always trying to figure out the best way to get what we want. The result of chasing this kind of freedom is we worry ourselves into unhealthy lifestyles and stress ourselves into early graves. Instead of chasing our own dreams for ourselves, full freedom in Christ takes the entire burden off of us. When we make it a point to join our will with God's, we consequently become free from worry and stress.

The burden of control can also accompany the pursuit of partial freedom. If my limited view of freedom includes having things just the way I want them, I naturally, then, become more controlling of others around me who threaten that image. In order for my circumstances to create the culture of freedom that I envision for myself, I have to control the people who interact within those circumstances. Controlling others is an impossible feat that we often take on in pursuit of partial freedom.

Full freedom frees us from the desire or the attempt to control others. When we make God's will our will, we realize that it's not up to us to control people, and we couldn't do it if

---

[1] Psalm 37:4 (ESV) - "Delight yourself in the Lord, and he will give you the desires of your heart."

we tried anyway. We may be able to control ourselves, but we can never control the intentions, words, or actions of others. Full freedom releases us from this dead-end activity that increases our anxiety and frustration.

Another unwanted consequence of partial freedom is it causes us to make unhealthy comparisons. We sometimes call it "keeping up with the Joneses." We may look at the lives of our friends or neighbors, our boss or colleagues, or even our enemies, and use their lives as a barometer for what we want for ourselves. We think that if we get what they have, then we can be as free and happy as they appear to be.

This is a huge deception for two reasons. First, their story is not your story. What is for them is not necessarily for you. Partial freedom can lead us to chase after things that aren't meant for us. The second reason this is a deception is because this person, no matter who he or she is, is not the standard-bearer. Whenever we compare something to something else that is not the standard, we are limiting the ability of that thing to achieve its full potential. Full freedom helps us to recognize that God is the standard, not any earthly person, no matter who the person is.

The Standard for Excellence

The Tabasco Hot Sauce company uses *le petit bâton rouge*, a "little red stick," to determine when peppers are ripe enough to pick. If a pepper doesn't match the fiery red color of the stick, then it isn't ready and still needs to remain in the field. Field workers carry the stick around so they can hold it up to each pepper. *Le petit bâton rouge* is their standard for excellence, the stick to which they compare each pepper.[2]

Each of us has our own versions of *le petit bâton rouge* that we use to assess our lives, decisions, qualities and relationships. Full freedom places Christ as our *le petit bâton rouge*, the standard by which we measure everything in our lives. Instead of looking to our friends for validation—or to find out if we're successful, or to figure out what we want for ourselves—when we're spiritually free, we look to God for all of these. We can only reach our full potential when we are measured against the correct standard, which is the life and person of Jesus Christ Himself.

The trouble is, it is very easy to make horizontal comparisons (person to person) rather than vertical comparisons (person to God) simply because we interact with other people every day, either in person, on TV, or on social media. Truthfully, horizontal comparisons often make us feel better about ourselves. We sometimes unintentionally lower our standards to something we might actually be able to reach when we compare ourselves to other people, and in this way, we settle for partial freedom. It would be like picking peppers based on the peppers around them, instead of based on the bright red stick. We would be risking a poor harvest because we can't tell if the peppers have reached their full potential.

If we're honest, it can be scary to consider replacing our friends and family as the standard because we know we can never reach the goal of a Godly standard on our own. But that's

---

[2] "The History of TABASCO® Brand." *TABASCO® Brand*, 25 May 2021, www.tabasco.com/tabasco-history/.

the beauty of joining our will with God's will for us. When we're living in obedience and harmony with God's will, God doesn't see our faults and flaws when He looks at us; He instead sees the irreplaceable sacrifice of His son Jesus Christ. And in that way, we get credit for reaching the standard. And, by the way, that's the only way we *can* reach God's standard: through the sacrifice of Jesus.

The most fulfilling effect that comes from full freedom is the freedom from sin. We are not suggesting that if you pursue full freedom instead of partial freedom, you will suddenly become a perfect person and you'll stop making mistakes. Paul speaks very directly against this idea in Romans 7 when he discusses the reasons he does things that he hates. Instead, what we are saying is that when you intentionally align yourself with Jesus Christ, He will free you from the grip of sin, including your love for it.[3] So while pursuing full freedom will free you from sin in one sense, it doesn't mean you will suddenly become perfect.

Maybe there are two equally accurate, but not equally significant, definitions of *perfection*. Yes, perfection means without blemish. But more importantly, particularly within the context of our relationship with Christ, perfection means constantly aligning with Christ.

King David in the Bible is a prime example. He was a man after God's own heart[4] not because he was perfect—he certainly didn't do everything right; in fact, he made just about every

---

[3] Romans 6:6-7, 14 (NIV) - For we know that our old self was crucified with Him, so that the body ruled by sin might be done away with, that we should no longer be slaves to sin—because anyone who has died has been set free from sin… For sin shall no longer be your master, because you are not under the law, but under grace.
[4] 1 Samuel 13:14; Acts 13:22

mistake you can make—but rather because he was always realigning himself with God. He's counted among the righteous because he was always ready to do what was necessary to align himself with God's will. And that's exactly what God wants from us; He wants us to pursue full freedom, and it can only be done *with Him*.

Planning with God

We can learn a lot about our alignment with God's will when we analyze how we plan our lives. Notice that at the end of the last section, we didn't say that full freedom can only be pursued "*in* Him"; we said "*with* Him." God doesn't merely want us to live *in* Him; He wants us to live *with* Him, and He wants to live *with* us.

In Revelation 21, John describes the new heaven and the new Earth that God creates after the second coming of Jesus Christ. In verse 3, John writes, "And I heard a loud voice from heaven saying, 'Behold, the tabernacle of God is *with* men, and He will dwell *with* them, and they shall be His people. God Himself will be *with* them and be their God'" (NKJV, emphasis added).

What God ultimately wants is an unbroken love relationship *with* us; He does not want to swallow us up and stamp out our uniqueness. God is not opposed to us having fun and enjoying ourselves; in fact, He's very much in favor of it (see "Eden Is A Playground"*)*.

Planning with God is making plans with God *as the goal*, rather than making plans with the goal of *using* God to help us accomplish *our* goals. When we're planning with God, God

Himself becomes the focus of our desires. So, planning with God is changing our focus from ourselves and what we want (or what we think we want) to the Person we're in a relationship with. All these desires that we have (comfort, happiness, pleasure, joy, peace, etc.) flow from our communion with God.[5] Skye Jethani, award winning author, puts it nicely in his book *With*: "In other words, God would cease to be how we acquire our treasure, and He would become our treasure."[6] This is a fundamental shift in our thinking, in where we place our desires.

If we ever feel reluctant to share our plans with God because we think He's going to say no, that's an indication that God is not our actual goal, and that our actual goal is ourselves. Planning with God means that our own desires are not our highest priority. Our first point of contact must be God if we are to plan with God. This also means that we give up the right to be in control of ourselves in some very meaningful ways. This idea is supremely counter-cultural. Planning with God means that we don't prioritize our ambition, our career, our bank accounts, or even our control over our trajectory. Planning with God means we admit that we don't have control and we need God's guidance.

Admitting that we don't have control doesn't mean we should do nothing about the situation we're in. We're not suggesting that we do nothing and wait for God to fix all of our problems for us. Instead, we're suggesting that if you make God

---

[5] Matthew 6:33 (NIV) - "But seek first His kingdom and His righteousness, and all these things will be given to you as well."
[6] Jethani, Skye. *With: Reimagining the Way You Relate to God*. Thomas Nelson, 2011, pg. 103.

your first point of contact with everything, you'll know what to do and when to do it.

It is natural to want to pursue your own desires, particularly when you grow up in a culture that prioritizes self over community, or smaller community over larger community. This kind of *groupish* thinking is very common. *Groupishness* is "the tendency on the part of groups to seek the most for the in-group without regard to the rights and needs of others, in order to advance the group's biased interests."[7] This is a form of socio-centric thinking: thinking that prioritizes those who are part of our immediate society or culture.[8]

Groupish thinking is self-serving; this means it cannot be an act of love, which is inherently *other*-centered. While there is nothing inherently wrong with wanting things for yourself, living your life based on this idea will prevent you from aligning your will with God's, and thus will limit your potential. God *is* love, so groupish thinking cannot fit into a life lived *with* Him. Living under this principle requires a complete shift in the fundamental way we think about our lives because groupish thinking is natural to us and living in God's will is not.

Oswald Chambers presents it this way:

> The natural life itself is not sinful. But we must abandon sin, having nothing to do with it in any way whatsoever. Sin belongs to hell and to the devil. I, as a child of God, belong to heaven and to God. It is not a question of giving up sin, but of giving up my right to myself, my

---

[7] Paul, Richard and Linda Elder. *The Miniature Guide to Critical Thinking Concepts & Tools 8th ed.* Roman & Littlefield, 2020, pg. 42.
[8] Ibid. p. 41

natural independence, and my self-will. This is where the battle has to be fought.[9]

In giving up our rights to ourselves and making God our treasure rather than treasuring our plans or our wants, we are truly aligning ourselves with God's will and by extension, unlocking the unlimited potential He has in store for us.

An important part of this is accepting that the barrier between us and God, sin, has been conquered. Therefore, sin has no power over us. Our identity is in Jesus, the one Who conquered sin for us through the power of God so that I could experience life with God now; not only when we get to Heaven, but right now. Heaven is not just a destination with huge mansions and streets of gold. The essence of Heaven is an unbroken relationship with God. Sin introduced a barrier that the sacrifice of Jesus removed. Now we can have the essence of Heaven while we're still on Earth.[10]

On Ridiculous Prayers

The boundaries of our prayers are determined by our relationship with God. Prayer is the ultimate gateway to a life of full freedom; it isn't just *communicating* with God, it's *communion* with God. When we pray in faith it's like we're playing in God's backyard. We are limitless because the God we serve has no limitations. The Bible says that God can do infinitely more than

---

[9] Chambers, Oswald. "The Opposition of the Natural." *My Utmost for His Highest.* December 9.
[10] Luke 17:20-21 (NLT): "One day the Pharisees asked Jesus, "When will the Kingdom of God come?" Jesus replied, "The Kingdom of God can't be detected by visible signs. You won't be able to say, 'Here it is!' or 'It's over there!' For the Kingdom of God is already among you."

we can think or imagine.[11] That means if we have an idea, even if it seems ridiculous or impossible, He can match and even surpass it.

Ridiculous prayers are prayers of faith because we don't see how they can possibly be answered.[12] Yet sometimes we pray with such little imagination, as if we don't believe in God's matchless power, or as if we feel like we're bothering Him with our requests. If we pray for things that we think are impossible, that will strengthen our relationship with God and help us destroy the box we often place God in.

Fundamental Changes

One type of prayer that many of us may consider ridiculous is a prayer for a change in character or some other fundamental change. People may sometimes hide behind the idea that "God made me this way," or "This is who I am," and so they make minimal effort, in prayer or in life, to change. Perhaps we follow this line of logic: God made me; God doesn't make mistakes; God made me the way I am for a reason; I should accept myself for who I am instead of trying to change. This is very tricky because there are ideas here worth holding on to, but the overall conclusion is faulty.

First, God did make you, and He did have a purpose in doing so. But God didn't make your *habits*; you did. God didn't manipulate the way your choices affected who you have become over the years. God started you on a journey with free will, which you have used to make the choices that ultimately made

---

[11] Ephesians 3:20 (NIV): "Now to him who is able to do immeasurably more than all we ask or imagine, according to his power that is at work within us"
[12] Hebrews 11:6a (KJV): "But without faith it is impossible to please Him."

you into the person you have now become. Saying "God made me this way" releases us from the responsibility of doing the difficult work of introspection and self-improvement.

It is also true that there are certainly traits that God put in all of us that we should lean into rather than change. But there are other traits that do not fit this description. So how do we know when to fight against our own nature, and when to accept who we are? The answer can only be found in relationship with God because God has a purpose for our lives that is not bound by our abilities. He gives us what we need even when we have doubts about ourselves.

When God initially called Moses to lead Israel out of Egypt at the burning bush, Moses reacted negatively to God's command. In Exodus 4,[13] we see Moses making excuses as he tried to resist the call of God. First, Moses worried that his Israelite kinsmen wouldn't believe that God had actually sent him. To alleviate this concern, God empowered Moses to perform great wonders. God assured Moses that God Himself would be with Moses during this whole process; God would help Moses perform this difficult task.

But Moses made another excuse, saying he has never been a good speaker. God said, "Who made your mouth? Don't worry, I'll help you." But Moses still resisted. Exodus 4:14 (NASB) is very revealing: "Then the anger of the Lord burned against Moses, and He said, 'Is there not your brother Aaron the Levite? I know that he speaks fluently. And moreover, behold, he is coming out to meet you; when he sees you, he will be overjoyed."

---

[13] Exodus 4:1-17

God provided what Moses *thought* he needed to fulfill God's command, but notice that God got mad at Moses first. Why did "the anger of the Lord [burn] against Moses"? Because Moses did not have enough faith in that moment to pray a ridiculous prayer. Instead, he tried to avoid his responsibility by making (valid) excuses. God gave Moses a command and immediately assured Moses that God Himself will be his help. But Moses still said, "I'm not good at that." This was the perfect opportunity for a ridiculous prayer, a prayer that said, "Change who I am so I can fulfill your purpose." But Moses did not pray a ridiculous prayer, and God got mad at him for it.

Three significant things happen in these verses. God didn't abandon Moses; God got His feelings hurt, and didn't hide that from Moses; and God took a step back because of Moses' doubts. God's plan was to stand beside Moses while Moses spoke to the Egyptians, but He changed His plans, and instead Moses stood with Aaron as Aaron spoke to the Egyptians. From our point of view, everything worked out in the end: the Israelites got their freedom and eventually made it to the Promised Land. But what would have happened with Moses' relationship with God and, therefore, God's relationship with the Israelites, if Moses had prayed a ridiculous prayer and trusted that God would give him what he didn't *think* he had, but actually did have because God was with him?

Maybe God gave Moses a speech impediment when he was younger *so that* when Moses became a great speaker later, everyone would marvel, thus giving Moses a perfect opportunity to point others to the goodness and power of God. Much like the lame man that Peter healed in Acts 3:1-10, or Lazarus' death in John 11, sometimes we lack so that we can be conduits that reveal God's character to others. If we lived with this mindset, what would we ask for in prayer?

Knowing when to lean in and when to change is completely based on the relationship we have with God.[14] We get confused and contradict ourselves when we try to figure these things out *without* God. There is no set formula other than knowing God personally and being in community with Him. But the key is that we shouldn't assume that because we have a particular trait, that it's a trait God wants us to cherish. Cherishing every trait reveals that, at least subconsciously, we believe that God cannot, or should not, change us.

We have seen this quite a bit in our careers as educators. I, Paul, once had a student who, whenever I told him anything predictive about himself, he would say, "You don't know what I got," which I understood to mean *you don't know me* or *you can't judge me*. I would say, "You don't have your book, do you?" He would say, "You don't know what I got." Then I would ask, "Do you have your book?" and he would reply, "No." Or I would say, "You didn't finish the required reading, did you?" He would say, "You don't know what I got." Then I would ask, "Did you finish the required reading?" and he would reply, "No."

One class period he was sitting at his desk, staring into space while the rest of the class was busy working on a peer review activity. Only students who had turned in a first draft were given a peer's assignment to review. His sitting there with nothing to do was an indication that he hadn't turned in his

---

[14] Mark 14:36 (ESV) - "And he [Jesus] said, 'Abba, Father, all things are possible for you. Remove this cup from me. Yet not what I will, *but what you will*'" (emphasis added).

work. I asked him, "Where is your paper?" despite knowing that he didn't have it. He got upset and stood up, issuing his usual refrain: "You don't know what I got." He left the classroom and never came back. I never saw him again. He didn't even drop the class; he just disappeared.

This student was intent on remaining *un*known to his professor. He wanted to be a mystery, and the idea that he wasn't a mystery was so detestable to him that he couldn't face me while knowing that I knew the truth. He didn't want to get better if getting better meant facing himself. Instead of admitting the simple truth that he didn't have his book or his assignment, he removed himself from the learning environment.

And this is the same danger we face when we choose to align ourselves with God. For many of us, it's a very scary process because we are so dedicated to what we want for our own lives. We've dreamt about it, planned for it, and made major life decisions based on it. Having that possibly threatened puts us in a natural defensive position. This natural response, though, highlights the significance of dying to ourselves daily.[15]

> Dr. John Nixon Sr. explains it this way:
>
> ...to know Jesus better is to know ourselves better. When we see Him clearly, we see ourselves with increasing clarity, and we suffer in comparison. We discover our beauty is vain, our strengths are weaknesses, and our self-confidence is unwarranted. The revelation of Christ casts our cultural values and

---

[15] Luke 9:23-24 (NIV): "Then he said to them all: 'Whoever wants to be my disciple must deny themselves and take up their cross daily and follow me. For whoever wants to save their life will lose it, but whoever loses their life for me will save it.'"

our self-esteem into judgment and forces us to choose between His beauty and our own self-image.[16]

His beauty is perfect, and when we choose His beauty every day, we can live lives that reflect that beauty.

Timeless Prayers (Not Time Travel)
Disclaimer: In this section, we want to explore an idea that is still a bit confusing to us. Our intention is to attempt to break free from ideas that are typically bound by time in an effort to draw closer to the One who is timeless. We may or may not do this well, but we still want to share our ideas with you.

There are a number of Bible stories we can cite as evidence that ridiculous things happen when we pray in faith. Job prayed for his children's sins *just in case* they may have cursed God in their hearts.[17] When King Solomon turned to idolatry, God promised to take the kingdom away from him as punishment. But God did not punish Solomon directly, for the sake of Solomon's father David, who was already dead.[18] There are even stories that demonstrate how the prayer of faith can affect the passage of time![19]

We live within the boundaries of time and, therefore, we think in linear terms. But it's limited to think that the God who *created* time is *bound* by time. The paradox of God's timelessness

---

[16] Nixon, John. *Redemption in Genesis: The Crossroads of Faith and Reason*. Pacific Press Pub. Association, 2011, p. 10.
[17] Job 1:5 (NLT): "When these celebrations ended—sometimes after several days—Job would purify his children. He would get up early in the morning and offer a burnt offering for each of them. For Job said to himself, 'Perhaps my children have sinned and have cursed God in their hearts.' This was Job's regular practice."
[18] 1 Kings 11:9-12
[19] Joshua 10:1-15; Isaiah 38:8

is encapsulated well when John the Baptist said in John 1:15b (NIV), "This [Jesus] is the one I spoke about when I said, 'He who comes *after* me has surpassed me because he was *before* me'" (emphasis added). In linear terms, this is a nonsensical statement, but this is God in His fullness both before and after; both then and now.

It's possible that *our past occurred the way that it did* because of our future prayers that God heard in His time.

In 2002, filmmaker M. Night Shyamalan released a film called *Signs* about an alien invasion and the Hess family's response to these events. At the climax of the movie, an alien is about to kill Graham Hess and his family with a poisonous gas. The alien is holding Graham's son Morgan, who is unconscious because of an asthma attack, and he sprays Morgan in the face with the gas. Graham's brother, Merrill, attacks the alien with a baseball bat, and the alien drops Morgan. Graham rushes Morgan outside and begins to do CPR on him, praying that the poison gas does not kill his son. In the end, Morgan's life-long defect, asthma, saves his life by preventing him from inhaling the poison gas.

This is a fictional scene, but it is a good example of how God's providence can work in our lives. Graham prays for something that God had already made plans for years before the alien invasion, and years before the prayer.

You might be thinking, "That's ridiculous." Good. That's our point.

In real life, our dad had a very similar experience in which God made plans for his future by using a car accident from his childhood to provide direction on whom he should marry (see "The Essence of God"). When you reflect on your own life, you may find similar instances where God put plans in place before you even started praying anything.

For us, time is past, present, and future. For God, every time is *now* because He is eternal.

Full Freedom is Ridiculous

We should also remember that as we grow with God, He guides our prayer life. This means He will correct things that need correction and will redirect where necessary. Our prayers will change the more we get to know Him and the more we spend time with Him.

> "Impossibilities cease to exist the moment we bring them to God in the name of Jesus Christ."

If He redirects our prayers, that's okay and preferable. The point is that the redirection should come from Him and not from ourselves. So, begin with the ridiculous and if He redirects, follow Him in that redirection. Begin, though, with intellectual curiosity and don't be afraid to pray for impossibilities.

The Bible says that we are limited by our *lack* of request—we don't have because we don't ask.[20] In other words, our belief that something is impossible creates the impossibility; it's a self-fulfilling prophecy and a form of self-sabotage. Impossibilities

---

[20] James 4:2-3 (NLT): "You want what you don't have, so you scheme and kill to get it. You are jealous of what others have, but you can't get it, so you fight and wage war to take it away from them. Yet you don't have what you want because you don't ask God for it. And even when you ask, you don't get it because your motives are all wrong—you want only what will give you pleasure."

cease to exist the moment we bring them to God in the name of Jesus Christ.[21]

We aren't talking about time travel; we aren't saying that if we pray that something in the past never happens that it suddenly wouldn't have happened. Even though God is infinite, He allows, through His permissive will, events to take place that have become history. Those things will not change—they are completed forever. This is easy for us to understand because we are only in the present and not in the past. In terms of time, we are one-dimensional creatures. We move only and ever forward in time, and there is no chance for us to change events that have already taken place. Again, we are not talking about traveling in time to change past events like the television show *Quantum Leap* or the movie *Back to the Future*.

But God is *not* one-dimensional in terms of time; He hears prayers *throughout* time. We pray now, God hears now, and acts on *then*—which is *His* now—within His permissive will.

When we recognize how God's hand has worked in our past—His grace, His mercy, His help, His love—it should motivate us to give thanks. Our prayer lives will change in meaningful ways when we start to pray for things that we literally think are impossibilities. They may be impossible for us, but nothing is impossible for God.[22] In fact, miracles are only miracles to us because miracles are what we consider impossibilities coming true.

---

[21] 2 Corinthians 1:20 (NIV): "For no matter how many promises God has made, they are "Yes" in Jesus Christ. And so through Him the "Amen" is spoken by us to the glory of God."
[22] Matthew 19:26; Luke 1:37

God, however, is just expressing His character in our lives; our lack of imagination in prayer sometimes makes this expression miraculous because we didn't think it could happen. Praying for impossibles, with the understanding that God's will reigns[23] and He will direct us in prayer, is a demonstration of faith and love, which means it is exactly what God wants from us.

How pleased would God be with us if our prayers were more ridiculous? How much more free would we be if our prayers were more ridiculous?

Aligning ourselves with God means shedding our old skin and putting on what God has created specifically for us. It is scary, and it is painful, but it's pain for a higher purpose. God is like a gardener with pruning shears, cutting away those parts of us that are harmful—even those parts that we may not view as harmful—so that we can grow to our fullest potential.

God doesn't want us to be stuck with our bad habits and negative traits. He wants us to be free, *fully* free, to enjoy our lives and relationships, our work and our play. Full freedom is not just doing whatever you want; it's also making all of yourself available to God—including your traits, emotions, thoughts and desires—for His own will. Full freedom can only be found in a meaningful, two-sided relationship with Jesus Christ.

---

[23] Luke 22:42 (NIV): "Father, if You are willing, take this cup from me; yet not My will, but Yours be done."

PRACTICAL STEPS FOR RIDICULOUS PRAYERS

1. Keep a Planning Journal and ask God to commune with you whenever you're writing in it.

   - Communicate with God first, before you start making plans, before you know what you want, before you are even totally clear on the options. This way you'll be planning *with* God as He's revealing Himself to you through the options that He shows you, through your desires, through Godly people who you ask for advice, etc.

   - Spend time listening as well as writing. Be intentional.

2. Take an emotional inventory.

   - Use an app like Mood Meter to help you identify your emotional patterns.

   - Pay close attention to the emotional investment you have with your obstacles. Instead of investing in feelings like dread, worry, and stress, be open to reimagining problems as a playground for God.

   - Be intentional about identifying fears in your prayers; what are you leaving out? What are you hiding from

God? Kill the power of those fears by writing them out and praying about them specifically.

- Identify where and on what you spend most of your time. You have the ability to affect your emotions by what you spend your time doing in relation to your daily issues and problems (see "The Protagonist Problem").

- Healthfully process (and move through) your emotions rather than planting yourself in them permanently. There's a difference between constantly rehearsing your problems (with friends, for example) and recognizing they exist while you bring them before God to see what He does with them.

3. Let God guide your prayer life. Use a prayer list that includes sections for

    - Intercession: add things that are focused on others.

    - Personal: add things that are focused on you.

    - Ridiculous: add things that should be impossible; things that only make sense through the power of Jesus Christ.

4. Study closely biblical characters who demonstrated full freedom in Christ (e.g. David, Peter, Paul, etc.). Take note of how they lived their lives (in their context) and think of

ways you can follow those same principles in your own life (and in your own context).

Comprehension Questions Based on the Chapter

1. What is the rhetorical situation (communicator, audience, and message) of the chapter, and why does this context matter?
2. What is the stated or implied thesis statement of the chapter?
3. What's the difference between *partial freedom* and *full freedom*?
4. What lesson can we learn from the way the Tabasco company chooses their peppers?
5. What does it mean to plan *with* God?
6. How can we tell if knowing God is *not* the ultimate goal of our plans?
7. What does it mean to pray ridiculous prayers?

Writing Questions

1. Consider the way you make the plans for your life. Do you plan things *with* God, do you make your plans and then ask God to bless them, or do you not involve God in your planning at all? What can you do to improve your planning with God?
2. Explain how giving up your right to yourself can help you to achieve full freedom.
3. Consider the situation with Moses and God in Exodus 4. How might a ridiculous prayer from Moses have made Israel's outcome with the Egyptians and the Promised Land even better?

4. Page 56 describes a fictional scene from the movie *Signs* that illustrates how God's providence is not limited to our concept of time. Think of a situation in your life or in a story you've heard or read that provides a similar illustration and briefly tell the story in your own words.
5. Read and annotate Exodus 4 (using the Logic Of if necessary). Golden Rule: every underline/highlight needs a corresponding comment.

CHRISTIAN ARTISTRY

God is a creative Person. When we align ourselves with God, our creativity grows beyond what we can even imagine or achieve on our own.

Habakkuk 2:1-3 (ESV)

I will take my stand at my watchpost and station myself on the tower, and look out to see what he will say to me, and what I will answer concerning my complaint. And the LORD answered me: "Write the vision; make it plain on tablets, so he may run who reads it. For still the vision awaits its appointed time; it hastens to the end—it will not lie. If it seems slow, wait for it; it will surely come; it will not delay.

Habakkuk was one of the Old Testament minor prophets, probably a contemporary of Jeremiah, Daniel, and Ezekiel. Although not much is known about the prophet himself, we do know some things about prophets in general. Prophets in the Bible functioned as God's messengers, usually to a particular people and for a particular period of time. In following God's commands, prophets frequently had to deliver difficult and unpopular messages and sometimes even act out dramatic scenes to get God's point across to His people. For example, Jeremiah smashed jars in front of an audience,[1] Ezekiel once

---

[1] Jeremiah 19:10 (NIV): "Then break the jar while those who go with you are watching…"

broke bread over human waste,[2] and Isaiah walked around naked for 3 years.[3] In all these cases, and more, the prophet was God's messenger, not just in word, but in deed. The prophet was like the actor, and God the director. Prophets are artists for God.

We don't often think about creativity as being part of God's character, although we see His creativity all throughout the Bible and the world. Because human beings are made in God's image, that means He placed in each of us creativity that can only come to its *fullest* potential through Him. When we align ourselves with God, our creativity grows beyond what we can imagine or achieve on our own. God wants us to be creative, and this short text from Habakkuk 2 outlines how we can be artists for God.

> "We don't often think about creativity as being part of God's character, although we see His creativity all throughout the Bible and the world."

Receive the Vision from God

God wants to be the director of our lives, and He wants us to live out His vision for our lives. The first lesson in becoming an artist for God is that the vision must be God's, not our own. In Habakkuk 2:2 (ESV), God is giving instructions: "And the Lord answered me: 'Write the vision; make it plain on tablets...'" God is commanding His prophet to take up a pen and write,

---

[2] Ezekiel 4:12 (NIV): "Eat the food as you would a loaf of barley bread; bake it in the sight of the people, using human excrement for fuel."
[3] Isaiah 20:3 (NIV): "Then the Lord said, 'Just as my servant Isaiah has gone stripped and barefoot for three years, as a sign and portent against Egypt and Cush...'"

clearly and on tablets. God, the director, is giving instruction to his actor. God tells Habakkuk to write down the vision that God Himself is about to give Habakkuk.

This is a similar concept to the one presented in Jeremiah 29:11 (KJV): "For I know the thoughts that I think toward you, saith the Lord, thoughts of peace, and not of evil, to give you an expected end." It's a beautiful verse that is brimming with positive upcoming prospects. Again, the thoughts, or the *plan*, are God's, not man's. God says that *He* is going to give Jeremiah hope and a future, not that *Jeremiah* is going to design it himself and chase it down. God does not ask us to "pursue happiness" as America's founding fathers inscribed. Instead, God asks us to rest in Him and to know peace and happiness as a result of that association. God gives us peace, hope, and a future, and they are all His idea, of His design, and of His execution! They are ours by way of gift, meaning we do not earn them. In order to receive these things, we must simply cooperate with God and accept them.

Re-defining Success

For God's followers, success cannot be limited to earning a particular salary or finally getting the business in the black. It cannot be about paying all of the bills on time or upgrading the house or the car. Success cannot be about working hard or even about working smart. For a follower of God, success is not based on achievement at all; it is about obedience to God's will.

This can be challenging for many of us because "obey" is almost like profanity in our Western, liberated society. We tend not to seek God's will for us; we instead make our own plans and then pray for God's blessing on the thing we have designed.

But if we plan first and pray second, we have done things out of order. The proper sequence is not to plan and then pray; it is to pray *while* planning so that you and God are working together throughout the whole process (See "Ridiculous Prayers"). For God's artists, success is not based on achievement, but obedience to God.

When we were children, our father, a pastor, accepted a call to leave his church in New York to become the pastor of a church in Los Angeles. At the time, California was known as the place where leaders in our denomination sent pastors who had gotten into trouble. Dad had a strong reputation in his community, so by accepting the call to California, he was risking the reputation he had cultivated through years of honest hard work for the Lord. But Dad felt called by God to accept the invitation to California, so he obeyed even though it didn't look like a wise career move.

God blessed our whole family because of Dad's obedience. Our years living in Los Angeles were refreshing and fruitful. We grew closer to each other as a family and to God, and everyone in our family experienced earthly success as well. We firmly believe that God's blessings came as a direct result of Dad's leading the family in obedience to God, in spite of the risk to his reputation and career. Dad understood that success is not based on achievement, but obedience, and we learned that same lesson through his example.

Whose Vision Is It?

In Habakkuk 2, notice that God does not say, "write your vision." The Christian Standard Version of the Bible says, "write this vision..." The New Living Translation says, "write my answer..." Habakkuk is merely a steward of the vision. He is not the vision's creator. If we are artists for God, we should follow the same standard of stewardship. The vision of artistic excellence, of success in the future, of creative prowess that God has given is *God's* vision. God is the one who gives visions, not man.

One of the surest ways to self-absorption and being unable to hear the voice of the Holy Spirit in our lives is replacing God's vision with our vision. In our modern, Western society, ambition is a virtue—something to strive for. In fact, it's part of "the American Dream." But misplaced ambition can be very dangerous. It can lead to self-righteousness, selfishness, covetousness, idolatry, impatience, just to name a few. When we make ambition a virtue apart from God, we develop traits that oppose Godly traits. These Godly traits are called the fruit of the Spirit: love, joy, peace, patience, kindness, goodness, faithfulness, gentleness, and self-control.[4]

Ambition is defined in Merriam Webster as "an ardent desire for rank, fame, or power." A more neutral definition from the same dictionary is, "desire to achieve a particular end." Without God, even when we start with the second definition, our ambition can easily slip to the first.

Ambition has its place, but, especially in the life of one of God's artists, the ambition must be submitted to the will of God. One Biblical scholar, Oswald Chambers, goes as far as stating that those who follow their personal ambitions actually cause Jesus pain!

---

[4] Galatians 5:22-23 (NLT): "But the Holy Spirit produces this kind of fruit in our lives: love, joy, peace, patience, kindness, goodness, faithfulness, gentleness, and self-control. There is no law against these things!"

Whenever we are obstinate and self-willed and set on our own ambitions, we are hurting Jesus. Every time we stand on our own rights and insist that this is what we intend to do, we are persecuting Him. Whenever we rely on self-respect, we systematically disturb and grieve His spirit.[5]

Ambition can take on a life of its own and lead us down paths that the Lord never intended, if all we're doing is chasing our dreams. As

> "What we do is important but *why* we do what we do is more important."

followers of God, we are called to something more than the obtaining of earthly renown and the acquisition of material possessions. Ambition, when not yielded to the will of the Lord, can be very dangerous.

To be clear, ambition is not sinful. We believe the intentions behind our actions are more important than our actions themselves. What we do is important but *why* we do what we do is more important.[6] Consider this admittedly extreme example. Both Adolf Hitler and Martin Luther King Jr. were men of great ambition, according to the second definition listed above, a "desire to achieve a particular end." But Hitler was ambitious for world domination while Dr. King sought world peace. In neither case was ambition itself the determining

---

[5] Chambers, Oswald. "How Could Someone So Persecute Jesus!" *My Utmost for His Highest*, Jan. 28
[6] 1 Samuel 16:7b (NIV): "The Lord does not look at the things people look at. People look at the outward appearance, but the Lord looks at the heart."

factor in the kind of person each man was; it was more about where their ambition was aimed.

The truth of the matter is, you do have talent. God has blessed you with a unique ability. You do something in a special way that nobody else can do. God has actually put power in your pen, or your brush, or your hands, or your voice, or your mind. Chambers wrote:

> Your mind is the greatest gift God has given you and it ought to be devoted entirely to Him. When you have thoughts and ideas that are worthy of credit to God, learn to compare and associate them with all that happens in nature—the rising and the setting of the sun, the shining of the moon and stars, and the changing of the seasons. You will begin to see that your thoughts are from God as well, and your mind will no longer be at the mercy of your impulsive thinking, but will always be used in service to God.[7]

The question is, will you wield this amazing power for God's glory, or will you simply use it to chase your own dreams? Put another way, whose dream are you chasing? Whose vision are you writing? If you're going to be an artist for God, you must first recognize that the vision you have is not your vision, but you are a steward of God's vision. Habakkuk was a steward of God's vision, which meant he only had one responsibility: to be obedient. God told Habakkuk exactly what to do, and all Habakkuk had to do was to carry out the instructions.

---

[7] Chambers, Oswald. "Is Your Mind Stayed On God?" *My Utmost For His Highest*, Feb. 11

God will make a way for you that your talent and your ambition alone cannot.

Use the Vision to Serve

At the end of Habakkuk 2:2 (ESV), the Bible says, "And the Lord answered me: 'Write the vision; make it plain on tablets, *so he may run who reads it*" (emphasis added). God was saying, "Write My vision plainly on tablets so that the person reading it can flee." In its historical context, God was giving Habakkuk a vision of warning for Judah. The tribe of Judah was morally and spiritually corrupt and had turned their backs on God. They were sacrificing children and animals to other gods and participating in idolatry; they had allowed the temple to fall to ruin, they oppressed the poor, and they ignored the legal system God had put in place.

God was giving them a warning before passing judgement on them, and Habakkuk's job was to deliver the warning. So, not only did the vision not *belong* to Habakkuk, but the content of the vision was not *about* Habakkuk either. The modern-day relevancy is that God's vision for you as a Christian artist is not about what you can get, but what you can give for the glory of God.

Followers of Jesus should be obsessed with giving.[8] We should be giving so much that other people wonder if we're crazy. We should be making fools out of selfish people because

---

[8] 2 Corinthians 8:7 - "But since you excel in everything—in faith, in speech, in knowledge, in complete earnestness and in the love we have kindled in you—see that you also excel in this grace of giving."

we *give* so much and we still *have* in abundance. And then, we should be pointing to our God saying He is the reason we even have anything at all. Jesus Christ lived His entire life on the principle of self-sacrificial love, but some of us give *Christian* a bad name with our selfishness. We love to take, and giving is an inconvenience. Neither of the previous mindsets is Christ-like.

Self-sacrificial love is very counter-cultural because Western culture emphasizes getting all you can. But not only is the idea of selfishness opposed to the Bible,[9] scientists are discovering that it is opposed to human nature and is unhealthy to the human body as well.

Love and Survival

One particularly poignant example of this scientific discovery is in a book called *Love and Survival* by Dr. Dean Ornish. In his book, Dr. Ornish reveals, from scientific experiments and observations, that emotional pain and violation have a negative effect on physical health, and that emotional support has a positive effect on physical health. He says:

> Anything that promotes feelings of love and intimacy is healing; anything that promotes isolation, separation, loneliness, loss, hostility, anger, cynicism, depression, alienation, and related feelings often leads to suffering, disease, and premature death from all causes.[10]

---

[9] 2 Corinthians 8:14 - "At the present time your plenty will supply what they need, so that in turn their plenty will supply what you need. The goal is equality…"
[10] Ornish, Dean. *Love & Survival: 8 Pathways to Intimacy and Health*. HarperCollins Publ., 2011, p. 2-3

That is to say, whatever you are suffering in your body, it is made worse when you suffer it in loneliness, in isolation, in rejection. And whatever you are suffering in your body, it will be made better if you are surrounded by people who love you and with whom you share an emotional safety and intimacy.

The book presents research that suggests healthy relationships are more important to physical health than any other factor of a healthy lifestyle. Having healthy, loving relationships is more important to your physical health than eating right, avoiding smoking, exercising, lowering your cholesterol, and it is even stronger than family history of disease. Dr. Ornish says that "infection may be a *necessary* but not sufficient prerequisite for illness to manifest when a person feels love and support."[11] When you are loved, your body is more likely to fight off sickness, even if you are exposed to infectious germs.

And it's not just receiving love that is healing. Dr. Ornish says that "giving and receiving love and intimacy are healing for both the giver and for the recipient."[12] So love is healing even if it only flows in one direction! If you treat people with love, it will benefit your physical health, even if they don't treat you with love in return. Of course, the ideal is that love flows both ways, but the fact is that love is healing even when it is unidirectional. Addiction specialists even conclude that the opposite of addiction is not sobriety. The opposite of addiction is positive connections with other human beings.[13]

---

[11] Ibid, p. 27
[12] Ibid, p. 29
[13] Weiss, Robert. "The Opposite of Addiction Is Connection." *Psychology Today*, Sussex Publishers, 30 Sept. 2015.

One particular study done at Johns Hopkins Medical School revealed shocking information about the incidence of cancer in men. Researchers performed a longitudinal study that spanned 50 years, where they used, among other things, a questionnaire called the "Closeness to Parents Scale" to assess the quality of the students' relationships to their parents. Through this study they found that "the best predictor of who would get cancer decades later was the closeness of father-son relationships earlier in life."[14] The father-son relationship was found to be more important than smoking, drinking, and even exposure to radiation.

In another study, strong social relationships were linked directly with longer life spans. Researchers noted that "those with close social ties and unhealthful lifestyles actually lived longer than those with poor social ties but more healthful behaviors. Not surprisingly, those who lived the longest had both close social ties *and* healthful behaviors."[15]

The three factors that were found to be the most important personality variables in coronary heart disease were hostility, cynicism, and suspiciousness.[16] More than any other factors, these are the things that cause disease and malfunction in the human body: loneliness, isolation, envy, racism, greed, hate, anger, self-centeredness. And these are the things that create optimization and can even reverse conditions in the human body: generosity, acceptance, kindness, forgiveness, loyalty, faithfulness, giving, other-centeredness.

---

[14] Ornish, Dean. *Love & Survival: 8 Pathways to Intimacy and Health.* HarperCollins Publ., 2011, p. 36
[15] Ibid, p. 42
[16] Ibid, p. 60

Even though Dr. Ornish, an atheist, and other scientists and researchers discover their information in a laboratory, science confirms what God has already declared in the Bible[17] (*see* "The Essence of God").

Since Dr. Ornish does not believe in God, he is baffled by his findings. He says that there is no doubt *that* this is true, but *why* it's true is still a mystery.[18] But followers of Christ know why it's true. God created human beings to be in positive, healthy, loving relationships with each other. God created us to love. And what is love? Love is other-centeredness. Love is "you first, me second" as Jesus Christ demonstrated continuously throughout His life. Learning to love is a process, and it all begins with our attention to God.[19] God created us to give, not to horde. So, we shouldn't be surprised by Dr. Ornish's findings. Is it so surprising that selfishness and greed are literally killing us? And that generosity and kindness can cure disease?

Writing His Vision

When you write God's vision, be careful that you write *His* vision and not *your* vision. Do not alter the vision God has given you so that you benefit from the bottom line. Write God's vision accurately, even if you are not directly in it, because, although the vision is not about you, God has promised that He

---

[17] Deut. 7:15; Prov. 3:7-8; Prov. 12:18; Prov. 15:13; Prov. 17:22; 1 Cor. 13:13
[18] Ornish, Dean. *Love & Survival: 8 Pathways to Intimacy and Health.* HarperCollins Publ., 2011, p. 22
[19] 2 Peter 1:5-6 (NLT): "In view of all this, make every effort to respond to God's promises. Supplement your faith with a generous provision of moral excellence, and moral excellence with knowledge, **6** and knowledge with self-control, and self-control with patient endurance, and patient endurance with godliness,..."

will reward your obedience to Him.[20] The pursuit of wealth, power, and fame apart from God are always opposed to God's perfect will. Oswald Chambers says, "A warning which needs to be repeated is that 'the cares of this world and the deceitfulness of riches,' and the lust for other things, will choke out the life of God in us."[21] God doesn't ask His artists to figure it out themselves, or to make sure they get theirs. He asks His artists to trust Him and to be obedient and He will take care of the rest.

By the end of the book, Habakkuk is a changed person. "He has learned to wait and trust in God, who works out all things for His glory."[22] Habakkuk's obedience to God's vision transforms Habakkuk himself, and his obedience is healing.

When we were children, our parents taught us this lesson explicitly as we grew up and matured. Dad once told us something that made us wonder if he was crazy. He said, "Whenever we are having financial trouble, I *increase* my giving to the church." We remember seeing this principle in action too. We would sometimes overhear Mom and Dad talking about some trouble to which the answer seemed to be more money, and then seeing Dad take a wad of cash out of his pocket and put the entire thing in the offering plate at church.

We were old enough to know simple arithmetic, and it didn't make any sense to us. Everyone knows that when you have less, you spend it more carefully, reserving the little that you have to make sure your family's basic needs are met. You

---

[20] James 1:25 (NLT): "But if you look carefully into the perfect law that sets you free, and if you do what it says and don't forget what you heard, then God will bless you for doing it."
[21] Chambers, Oswald. "Look Again and Think." *My Utmost for His Highest*, Jan. 27
[22] "Introduction to Habakkuk." *ESV Bible*, https://www.esv.org/IntroductiontoHabakkuk/

only give when you have extra, especially to church because God doesn't need our money—He already has the cattle on 1,000 hills.[23] But over the years, as we observed our parents interact with their money, we found that the promise of Psalm 37:25 (ESV) is true: "I have been young, and now am old, yet I have not seen the righteous forsaken or his children begging for bread."

Simply put, God takes care of those who trust Him, and to trust Him we have to give up the idea that we are responsible for taking care of ourselves. God never asks us to only take care of ourselves; He asks us to take care of *others*. Followers of God are givers, not hoarders.

Does that mean you shouldn't plan ahead or handle your responsibilities? Does that mean you'll always be comfortable or you'll never miss a meal? Does that mean every bill will be paid on time and your car will always have gas in it? Does that mean you'll never be jobless, or you'll never be homeless? No! But it does mean you never have to be *hope*less because you trust that the promises of God are true.

As an artist for God, set in your mind that you will write His vision accurately, even though the vision may include an uncomfortable period, and even though the vision may not be about you. God will use your faithfulness as an example to bring someone else into the Light of His love and salvation, and He will not abandon you in the process. In the end, you will find, like Habakkuk, that obedience to God is in itself holistically healing.

---

[23] Psalm 50:10 (NIV): "for every animal of the forest is mine, and the cattle on a thousand hills."

Be Patient

Habakkuk 2:3 (ESV) says, "For still the vision awaits its appointed time; it hastens to the end—it will not lie. If it seems slow, wait for it; it will surely come; it will not delay." The language of the verse indicates that the vision may not be fulfilled immediately, but instead, it will be fulfilled at the right time. God tells His artist to "wait" for the vision to be fulfilled, because it is going to happen. This may be the most difficult thing for one of God's artists to do because, as we mentioned before, you actually have talent. Your gifts are clear and obvious, and there are probably people around you who are benefitting from their gifts right now. There may even be someone who you perceive as less talented than you are who seems to be more successful from a traditional (e.g., moneymaking, prestige, etc.) standpoint. Have you ever thought something like this: "Why is Joe making more money than I am? I'm better than him at this!"

We believe this is a somewhat normal reaction for an artist, but God's artists must be held to a different standard. We must be followers of God first, and artists second. We must respond to situations and people from a Godly perspective, even and especially as it relates to the field of our gifts.

God's vision has a specific release date, and it is not for us to question what is happening in the meantime. We must be careful to avoid the pitfall of measuring our success by the success of others. Remember, success for God's artists is defined by obedience to the command of God, not by the amount of money we are making or the number of projects we get funded. And we certainly should not measure our own success according to the amount of money *someone else* is making or the number of projects *someone else* gets funded. In the text, God gave His vision to Habakkuk and to Habakkuk alone. Based on this and many other examples, you must understand that your task is specific to you, and God has a different task for a different person.

As people, and especially as Christians, we must be wary of the *horizontal* comparison: we must be careful about when and why we compare ourselves to other people, keeping in mind that other people are not our standard. Instead, we must make it a point to engage in *vertical* comparisons: we should look up to Him who is to be our standard for everything, especially success (*see* "Ridiculous Prayers").

When we are obedient to the will of God, we should expect push back from others. Western culture is at odds with the ways of Christ; this is why so many of the principles we learn in the Christian context are *counter*-cultural. The concept of other-centeredness is counter-cultural. The concept of letting someone else, *anyone else*, decide what success looks like for you is counter-cultural. The concept of not measuring our success according to other people in the field is counter-cultural. In fact, the Bible guarantees trouble in this life, not ease. James 1:2-4 (NKJV) says, "My brethren, count it all joy when you fall into various trials, knowing that the testing of your faith produces patience. But let patience have its perfect work, that you may be perfect and complete, lacking nothing."

James 1:2-4 does not say to count it all joy "if" you fall into trials; it says "when" you fall into trials. Trials are coming, and many times those trials are of Godly design. Sometimes God brings trouble to test us; sometimes to heal or restore us; and sometimes to prove a point.

An important part of the James text above is "let patience have its perfect work." This suggests that patience is required for emotions that are difficult to process or live through, and we shouldn't run from negative emotions. Through the power of God, though, we can honor the emotional responses that God has placed in us without letting them control our lives, and we can process them in healthy ways. Sometimes that process looks like physical exercise or journaling; sometimes it looks like speaking with a licensed professional or mental health care provider. It could be a combination of all of these and other ideas. Our perspective of negative emotions can help us grow when we face them and see them as opportunities to draw closer to God.

Whatever the reason for the trouble that requires patience, one thing is sure: trouble is coming. And when it comes, what will you do? Will you give up on the pursuit of God's dream for you because it is taking longer than you thought it would? Will you be deterred by a big bump in the road? Or will you maintain the courage of your conviction and stay the course until you reach the goal that God has set out for you? Admittedly, this can be very difficult because sometimes God does send trouble so that we will change the course of our actions. But God typically sends trouble to change our course when we have not been obedient to Him in the first place.

If God has convicted you of a particular course, if the dream you are pursuing is in fact God's dream, do not give up on the dream until it has been fulfilled. Remember that many people do not want you to achieve God's dream; there are opposing forces at work that will block your path simply *because* you are trying to do the will of God.

Your path to success as a Christian artist will not be without trouble, and there is a very good chance that the desired outcome will not be immediate. But we learn from the text in Habakkuk that, because the outcome is not immediate, it does not mean the result has been delayed. God promises that the outcome will be realized when He wants it to be. So, while the outcome might seem like a delay to us because it is not immediate, the reality is that God's timing is within the context of the universe and the result will be realized according to His perfect schedule. But, as God's artists, we must have faith in God and in His wisdom.

Habakkuk learned his lesson. He began the book complaining to God about the situation, and he ended the book praising God for His goodness and mercy. Habakkuk learned that God's justice and faithfulness were way beyond Habakkuk's ability to comprehend. And that's why, in order to be God's artist, Habakkuk had to submit himself to God's will, to be willing to be used as a tool in the hand of the Master Artist.

If you seek to be an artist for God, submit yourself to the Master Artist. Dedicate your gifts back to Him, and watch Him use you for His glory. He will take you to higher heights than you ever imagined were possible—only if you yield your will to His.

Practical Steps for Christian Artistry

Submit your preferences to God.

1. Take some time to decide what you really want for yourself. What are your biggest goals for your talents? Admit that you have preferences and desires of your own. Then, pray to God and ask Him to do what *He* wants to do with you, even if it means not getting the thing that you most want from your talents.

   - Remember that there is no sin in merely having a preference. There is nothing wrong with wanting things for yourself. The problem many of us have is not that we want things, it's that we ignore the voice and direction of God in our pursuit of the things we want. We must train ourselves to obey God even when obeying Him doesn't lead us where we prefer to go.

2. Target a specific person or group to uplift with your talents.

   - Ask God to reveal to you whom He wants your talents to minister to. Be open to sharing your talents with people with whom you don't already have a close relationship.

   - This is a great opportunity to practice sacrificial giving. Give to your target group or person without charging them. And give your best work! Don't merely donate the throwaway stuff that you would never sell anyway.

3. If it seems to be taking a long time, focus on the path, not the destination.

    - This might seem counter-intuitive, but sometimes focusing on the goal can be disheartening because the goal seems so far away. Instead, focus on the step you are on in the process, or the next step you have to take. Turn your attention to the smaller thing, and note that baby steps are still steps.

    - If the steps you are taking are within God's will, the destination will take care of itself. Pray for the strength to be obedient to God's will every day—or even several times a day—and follow through with it so that you are sure that you don't have to worry about reaching the proper destination.

4. Focus on vertical comparisons (you and God) rather than horizontal ones (you and someone else)

Comprehension Questions Based on the Chapter

1. What is the rhetorical situation (communicator, audience, and message) of the chapter, and why does this context matter?
2. What is the stated or implied thesis statement of the chapter?
3. Explain how self-sacrificial love is counter-cultural.
4. What is a spiritual definition of "success"?
5. Why is *why* we do what we do more important than *what* we do?
6. Explain why the authors say Christians should be obsessed with giving.
7. Why do the authors say it can be dangerous to measure success based on the success of others?

Writing Questions

1. Explain how God's love (i.e other-centeredness) is *scientifically* proven to be healthier for the human body than anything else.
2. What are some of the potential benefits of writing God's vision instead of your own? What are some of the potential dangers of writing your own vision instead of God's?
3. Apply the principles of this chapter to a person who does not consider themself an artist. What are some of the relevant takeaways for a non-artist?
4. Explore the importance of controlling your personal ambition. How can ambition be a two-edged sword,

having either positive or negative outcomes depending on how you relate to it? What can you do to make sure your ambition works for God?

5. Read and annotate Habakkuk 2 (using the Logic Of if necessary). Golden Rule: every underline/highlight needs a corresponding comment.

EDEN IS A PLAYGROUND

God is a fun-loving Person. God wants us to have fun, and it is evident in His original plan for humanity.

Genesis 2:8 (NASB)
The Lord God planted a garden toward the east, in Eden; and there He placed the man whom He had formed.

The Christian lifestyle is not often thought of as a fun lifestyle. The Bible never records God saying to His prophets, "Deliver this message, and have fun with it," or Jesus saying to His disciples, "Go heal those people, and enjoy yourselves!" In fact, it might seem like following God is not supposed to be fun.

The Bible promises trouble in this earthly life on more than one occasion and in many, perhaps even most, cases, those who are doing the will of God don't look like they are having very much fun. Going back to Egypt to confront Pharaoh about setting all of the slaves free was not Moses' idea of fun.[1] Taking command of the Israelite army so he could defeat the enemy with only 300 men was not Gideon's idea of fun.[2] Going to Nineveh to deliver God's message of warning was not Jonah's

---

[1] Exodus ch. 3
[2] Judges ch. 6

idea of fun, which was why he fled to Tarsus.[3] Selling all he owned and giving to the poor so that he could follow Jesus was not the rich young ruler's idea of fun, which was why he didn't bother doing it.[4] No, fun is not the calling of those who follow God.

Or is it?

Although it may seem as though fun is not high on God's list of priorities for His children, there is evidence that fun was part of God's original plan for humanity. Two clues of this plan are found in Genesis 2:8 (NASB): "The Lord God planted a garden toward the east, in Eden; and there He placed the man whom He had formed." This text shows us that fun is part of the package when we decide to follow God.

The Intentional Nature of God

The language of Genesis 2:8 describes God's intentionality. The text uses three words that indicate God did what He did on purpose, which means He had a reason for doing what He did. The words are: *planted*, *placed*, and *formed*.

The third word in the list may be familiar to us in this context. Many preachers talk about how God spoke things into existence during the creation week, but when it came to humanity, He chose to use His hands; God *formed* man from the dust of the ground, then *formed* woman from the man's rib. It is a strong point about the elevated importance of humanity in the creation narrative. In the same way God said, "let there be light"

---

[3] Jonah ch. 1
[4] Luke 18:18-23

and there was light, God could have said, "let there be man," and there would have been man. But He saw a reason to create man differently. He chose not to *speak* man; He chose to *sculpt* man. The clear implication is that the portion of creation that was *formed* is more important to God than the portion of creation that was merely spoken. God took particular care in some cases to demonstrate how special His creation was.

Less often, however, do we discuss how God also used His hands to create man's living quarters. God did not speak the garden into existence, He *planted* it. This act carries the same implication of importance that using His hands for the creation of man carries. God *planted* the garden because He wanted it to have a special purpose and meaning. Indeed, the garden was to be especially cherished by man, so God took care in *planting* it.

God's intentionality is also demonstrated in the use of the word *placed*. God did not push the man in a general direction, and God did not tell the man to go wherever he wanted. God was intentional about where man was to be. God wanted there to be a garden so He *planted* one, and He *placed* the man whom He had *formed* inside of the garden because He had a reason for wanting man to be there. Genesis 2:15 (NIV) says: "The Lord God took the man and put him in the Garden of Eden to work it and take care of it."

> "...the garden was to be especially cherished by man, so God took care in *planting* it."

This concept of being placed where one is wanted has recently been illustrated for me, Paul, in my life. My wife and I recently had our first child, a son we named Theodore. At the beginning of his life, Theodore had not yet learned the skill of mobility: he didn't walk or crawl. Up until that point, he rolled over but only from his stomach onto his back; he didn't know how to roll over from his back onto his stomach. Theodore was completely dependent on his mother and me for his mobility. He only went places where he was taken, and he only had things that he was given.

If you think about it, Theodore was at that time always in his parents' will for him, if only because he had no other choice at that point in his life. If we put him in his crib, he stayed in his crib until we took him out. If we put him on his activity mat on the floor, the best he could do was roll over once onto his back; but he would still be on the activity mat until we moved him somewhere else. Theodore was always intentionally placed where we wanted him to be.

"But Theodore was a baby," you say. "I don't want to be limited to the places where someone else wants me to be. I want to go my own way." And perhaps that is the problem. If my wife and I, being fallen, sinful parents, did our best to only place Theodore in positive situations and environments, then how much more will God, being perfect and loving, make sure that His will for us is for our own good? We should trust God with our decisions, both great and small, because obedience to God is the only true freedom in this life (*see* "Ridiculous Prayers"). In Matthew 18, Jesus admonishes His disciples to become more like children, humbling themselves before Him instead of seeking position and acclaim amongst each other. It would be wise for us as followers of Christ to fight against our own will, and to be willing to be placed where He wants us to be.

This first clue from Genesis 2:8 about God's intentionality does not surprise us because we know from other Bible stories[5] and from our lives that God is a God of order who does things for a purpose. It was God's purpose that there would be a garden, and that the man would be in the garden, so He *planted* and He *placed* whom He had *formed*.

The Meaning of the Garden of Eden

We also know that fun was part of God's original plan because the Bible says that the garden is in Eden. That's why it's called "The Garden of Eden." But don't think of Eden as a place so much as a substance. Yes, Eden is a physical location in the story, but in most Old Testament narratives people and places were named based on what they were made for, or their purpose. For example, *Adam* in Hebrew is translated to *man* in English. So, Adam's name was, essentially, Humanity, because that's what he was at the time of his creation. *Eve* in Hebrew is translated *to breathe*, or *to live* in English. So, God created humanity, then He enabled humanity to live by creating Eve. Purpose and name are synonymous in the context of this Old Testament story. Thus, Eden is a physical location, but it's called Eden because of its purpose.

---

[5] Some examples include: Genesis ch. 15; Luke 7:11-17; John 9:1-12

Well, what was the purpose of Eden? It can be found in the meaning of the name *Eden*. Eden means *delight* or *pleasure*, which was the purpose of the location and everything in it. That is to say that everything in Eden was designed for the pleasure of Adam and Eve, or humanity. Imagine if you had a garden with plants in it, and all of the plants were roses. It would be, not only acceptable, but appropriate and correct for you to say you had a rose garden, or a garden of roses. If you had such a garden, it would not be possible for you to enter the garden without being surrounded by roses. That's exactly what God intended when He *planted* the garden in *Eden* and *placed* the man there.

> "Eden means delight or pleasure..."

God named the man *Humanity;* He named the woman *To Breathe;* and He named their home *Pleasure*. God's intent here is clear. God's original intent for humanity was that we would be surrounded by pleasure; that everything we experienced would be pleasurable to us. God planted a garden in the middle of delight, in the center of pleasure, and placed the man and the woman there to live and to care for it.

The Fun of Following God

Let's take it a step further.

When God placed Humanity in Pleasure, Humanity was both surrounded by delight *and* perfectly within the will of God. So, doing the will of God should be delightful; following God's commands is supposed to be pleasurable. Put another way, humanity was made to experience delight through doing God's will. In other words, obedience to God is intended to bring us delight. God's will for us is intended to be pleasurable, and the boundaries that He places in our lives are meant to enhance that pleasure (*see* "Ridiculous Prayers").

But are *pleasure* and *fun* the same thing? For the connection between these two terms, we need to look no further than the dictionary. *Pleasure* is defined in the New Oxford American Dictionary (NOAD) as "a feeling of happy satisfaction and enjoyment" and "an event or activity from which one derives enjoyment." From these definitions, pleasure and fun aren't necessarily the same thing. For example, finishing a task at work, doing chores around the house, or completing a homework assignment might be pleasurable, but they are not necessarily fun. But the NOAD also includes this definition for pleasure: "enjoyment, entertainment, contrasted with things done out of necessity." This definition of pleasure that intentionally contrasts *pleasure* with things done out of necessity sounds a lot more like what we would call *fun*. This definition helps clarify the idea that Eden was not only a place where Adam and Eve completed necessary tasks, but was also a place to have fun.

> "...doing the will of God should be delightful; following God's commands is supposed to be pleasurable."

The new couple must have had chores, and we suggest that those chores were fun because Adam and Eve were more focused on their relationship with each other and God than they were on the tasks themselves. Someone might find completing chores pleasurable, but, to us, pleasure is not the purpose of chores; although for Adam and Eve, it was. Chores for us often get in the way of our pleasure, but for Adam and Eve, their chores were one way to have fun.

Fun in God's Service

Does that mean that if you are not having fun, then you are not serving God? Or that we should pursue fun at all costs, because that was God's original intent? No, it does not. We have to remember what happened at the time when sin entered humanity. When Adam and Eve ate the forbidden fruit, the only thing that changed was their *perception* of their reality. Adam and Eve were not more naked after sin, but they were ashamed of their nakedness after sin. God's character was not suddenly sinister, yet Adam and Eve were now afraid of God. God's goodness never wavered, yet the man and his wife hid from their Creator. As a result of their disobedience, humanity lost the ability to determine with complete accuracy and confidence what was good and what was not good. In other words, because of sin, we don't always know what's good for us.

And we still have this problem. As a result, we cannot be completely trusted to seek our own fun. Left unchecked long enough, our idea of fun will become harmful, painful, dangerous, evil, selfish, and dirty. God wants us to have fun, but we must seek our fun in Him, because fun in Him is always safe. Remember, when they were in Eden, Adam and Eve were simultaneously surrounded by pleasure and in the center of God's will. It was always in the context of His will that God intended for Adam and Eve to have fun.

So what about having fun in God's will? Does seeking fun in God mean that everything you do in God will be fun? Does it mean that following God's purpose for your life will make you feel like you're constantly in the Garden of Eden? The answer to that question is certainly no. One of the consequences of sin entering humanity is that not everything we do in Him will be fun.

Because of sin, everyone will have trouble in this life, whether or not they are following God. It's the nature of human existence. This is part of what it means to be *shapen in iniquity*.[6] The statement is not only about humanity being sinful, but also about the world around them being sinful. This world is messed up and everyone who lives in it is going to experience that reality. Trouble is inevitable.

So how do we get to the fun? If trouble is guaranteed in this life and fun is not, then why even try? The answer is oxymoronic: it is an obvious secret. God created fun, and God created us to live in fun. Who better than God to lead us into activities and situations that will amuse and entertain us? If God's peace "surpasses all understanding,"[7] then His fun passes all understanding too.

God's peace does not make total sense to us. When we are submitted to God's will, we experience God's peace at times when, by all accounts, we should be stressed out and worried. God's fun is in the same category. When we are cooperating with the Holy Spirit, we will find ourselves having fun, not only when we're playing games and watching movies, but also when we are feeding the homeless, doing mission work, loving each

---

[6] Psalm 51:5 (KJV): "Behold, I was shapen in iniquity; and in sin did my mother conceive me."
[7] Philippians 4:7 (ESV): "And the peace of God, which surpasses all understanding, will guard your hearts and your minds in Christ Jesus."

other, and forgiving those who have wronged us. All these things should bring us pleasure and delight. For instance, if you haven't actively participated in a service project of some kind, talk to someone who has. There is a very good chance that the person involved in service had fun in the midst of whatever outward conditions were in place, especially if those conditions were less than ideal.

Pleasure in God's Will

I, Paul, spent a year in South Korea as a missionary English teacher, and while I was there, I learned the truth behind having fun in God's will. First, I left a job that I truly loved to undergo this missionary experience. At this job, I had been developing a reputation for being a highly skilled worker, I made a respectable salary, and I was continually given opportunities for professional development and career advancement. I left, not because there was anything wrong with the job, but because I heard the call of the Holy Spirit.

As a missionary, I did not receive a salary for my work; I only received a stipend. I was on the opposite side of the world from almost everyone I knew. The only other people in my school who spoke fluent English were South African—I was the only American at my school when I got there. The food was different, the language was different, the pay was different, and the people were different. And to top it off, the hot water in my apartment did not work for the first month that I was there, and I arrived in January. So I had to take cold showers during the winter in a strange new country for very little money while surrounded by strangers.

Sure, it was a difficult time. However, not only did I grow much closer to God and learn a lot about myself and what I can handle during that year, but it was without a doubt one of the most fun years of my life. I made some great friends among the South Korean students and the other missionary teachers; we had a blast together taking in the local culture and traveling to neighboring cities and countries; and, believe it or not, I was even able to save some money while I was there.

Everything that might have been considered challenging or difficult while I was in South Korea that year turned out to be not just for the good of my soul, but a real pleasure and a lot of fun. And this feeling of fun was not something that I discovered later. I was able to truly enjoy the fun moments in South Korea in real time, as they were happening, because I had submitted my will to God before I even left my previous job. When we are following God's will, we can trust Him to give us the things that will fill our souls, namely peace, joy, happiness, and yes, fun.

Some of my, Clarise's, favorite memories are from moments in my childhood where my parents were really struggling for money. When we moved from California, where we were financially comfortable, to Massachusetts, my mother didn't have a job for the first year, so we struggled financially. That Christmas, my parents didn't have money to buy us many Christmas presents. I got a jump rope and a coloring book, and my brothers each got matching hats and gloves and they got a corded phone to share (cell phones were not yet popular or affordable).

Neither I nor my brothers remember feeling disheartened or troubled by this at all, however. In fact, it remains my favorite Christmas memory because it was the most simple

Christmas I recall ever having. Our lack of financial security removed the distractions of asking for what we wanted, anticipating huge amounts of gifts, and focusing our attention on ourselves. Instead, we were grateful that my parents got us anything at all, and we were quite happy to just spend time with one another. Essentially, our Christmas present was each other that year.

This is God's intention: our relationships with one another are supposed to be full of pleasure. Sometimes, the fun we seek gets in the way of God's intention for the pleasure in our lives. When those desires are stripped from us or are unattainable, we have an opportunity to return to God's original plan for our pleasure.

As beings created in the image of God, we are not totally inept in the area of finding fun. A lot of human fun is perfectly harmless, and some of it is actually very good for us. Things like exercise, reading and study, and spending time with friends and family come to mind as things that are both very fun and very healthy. The problem is we do not know beginning from end, and our perspective is skewed anyway. So even the things that are healthy and fun can be abused and turned into curses when we don't seek God's wisdom in all that we do. If you exercise improperly, you could injure yourself. If you spend too much time studying and reading, you will miss out on the development of important social skills. And if you spend too much time idly hanging out with your friends and family, you won't become a very productive member of society.

If we make it a habit to seek fun as an end in itself, we will eventually do it wrong. Because of the built-in misconceptions we have as a result of sin, fun can have many negative and disastrous side effects, even when it seems innocuous or even positive at first. Left to our own devices, we will eventually get hurt, or we will hurt someone else with what we think of as fun. The key is to prioritize God's will, and to be sure we are engaging in activities that are reflective of the character of God as it is revealed in the person of Jesus Christ. Matthew 6:33 (ESV) says, "But seek first the kingdom of God and His righteousness, and all these [fun] things will be added to you."

Practical Steps for Fun in God's Will

Here is a short 3-step process to help you to find the fun in God's will for your life. As always, honesty is key to this exercise. If you are not honest with yourself before the Lord, then this cannot and will not work for you.

1. Make a list of the things that you enjoy doing, whether they are things that you actually get a chance to do, or things that you wish you could do more often. The list is not so much about what you actually do, it is more about what you like to do. So include things on the list that you do rarely, but that you do when you can because you enjoy doing them.

2. Once your list is complete, prayerfully go through the activities one by one and determine if that activity is an accurate reflection of the character of Jesus Christ. You may need help with this step, and if you do, we encourage you to involve your spouse, your best friend, your closest sibling, or your counselor. Run your ideas by another Christian person who has a similar value system to you and who will tell you the truth.

3. For every activity you identify that is questionable or is clearly not something God is happy with, pray for deliverance from it. If you stop engaging in that activity, that is very good; if you stop wanting to engage in that activity, that is even better. If you replace that activity with something that is in God's will, that is best. Ask God to change your desires so that you only want to do what He

wants you to do. And ask Him to not only give you the sense of fun that you sincerely desire, but to attach that feeling of fun to the things He wants for you.

Comprehension Questions Based on the Chapter

1. What is the rhetorical situation (communicator, audience, and message) of the chapter, and why does this context matter?
2. What is the stated or implied thesis statement of the chapter?
3. According to the authors, which one of God's characteristics is revealed in the words *formed*, *planted*, and *placed* in Genesis 2:8?
4. What is the significance of the definition of *Eden*?
5. What is the connection between the words *pleasure* and *fun*?

Writing Questions

1. Analyze the logic that helps the writers conclude that God wants us to have fun in our lives.
2. Explain the connections between the words *planted*, *placed*, and *formed* in this chapter. What do those words refer to, and what is the significance of their relationship to each other?
3. Think of a time in your life when you did not have everything you wanted, but still had a good time. What was your source of fun in that instance? In your situation, was your *lack* in any way helpful to the fun you had at the time?
4. Consider two or three people, places, products, etc. that you think are named well. How do the names help to illustrate the essence or the purpose of the person or

thing? How can you use the name of a thing to communicate the purpose of that thing?

5. How can following God's will actually be more fun than going your own way? Think of one or two realistic scenarios in which it would be more fun to do things God's way.
    - Note: we're not talking about being healthy or getting to heaven. We're talking about having fun right now on Earth while following God's will.
6. Read and annotate Genesis 2 (using the Logic Of if necessary). Golden Rule: every underline/highlight needs a corresponding comment.

SPIRITUAL DIALYSIS

God is a community-minded Person. The church is supposed to function in the world the way Jesus did while He was on Earth.

John 15:5 (NIV)
I am the vine; you are the branches. If you remain in me and I in you, you will bear much fruit; apart from me you can do nothing.

Spiritual excellence is a goal of the Christian church. To be spiritually excellent, the Church and its members have to aspire to love like Jesus loves: completely and unabashedly. To mirror this love, we must love vertically—upward toward God—and horizontally—side-by-side toward other people. The image of a cross depicts this concept very well. You can perform an Internet search of "cross" right now and see countless images of a lowercase "t"; two boards intersecting one another. The vertical board is longer than the horizontal board, representing our desperate need to stay connected to God above all other things. But the boards are also stuck to each other, and you can't have one without the other. Representing this kind of love on Earth takes supernatural power.

To God, excellence is a matter of love. Spiritual excellence includes both forgiveness and accountability.

Luke 17:3-4 (AMP) says:

Pay attention and always be on guard [looking out for one another]! If your brother sins and disregards God's precepts, solemnly warn him; and if he repents and changes, forgive him. Even if he sins against you seven times a day, and returns to you seven times and says, 'I repent,' you must forgive him [that is, give up resentment and consider the offense recalled and annulled].

There is an equation here: spiritual excellence = accountability + forgiveness + patience.[1] When we do all of this, we free people from the feelings of guilt and reconcile them both to God and to the community.

Formula For Success

One church demonstrated this formula well when one of its young Christian members got pregnant before she was married, an infraction in that church community. She was an active member of her church and she felt very guilty about her situation. She went to the pastor in shame and confessed her wrongdoing. The pastor prayed with her and planned to meet with her again in a few days. During the days between meetings, the pastor prayed to God, asking for the right words to say and the right action to take in the young woman's case because he understood the value of keeping her within the loving community, which is an important responsibility of the church.

---

[1] Accountability - "If your brother sins... solemnly warn him"
Forgiveness - "... if he repents and changes, forgive him."
Patience - "If he sins against you seven times a day... you must forgive him."

Impressed by the Holy Spirit, the pastor met again with the young woman and outlined his plan. The young woman was excited about the pastor's plan and agreed to it completely.

The next week in church, the plan was put into action. The pastor called the young woman forward to stand before the congregation. He explained the situation to the church, then told them how they would move forward as a church community in this case. The young woman was removed from all offices she held for the term of her pregnancy. She was not allowed to serve in church while she was pregnant, although she was still allowed to attend services. Her censure was to officially end when the baby was born, and at that time she would be fully reinstated as an active member, able to serve and to hold positions once again. This also meant that the new baby would be born free from the judgment of the community and free from the guilt of the mother. This process also strengthened the bond between the new mother and the church, another powerful benefit for the child.

In this process, the pastor led the young woman in the full course of reconciliation with God and with the church community. Her own conscience had convinced her to confess, and she was corrected. But the church did not discard her; instead, they more fully embraced her and made it clear that the purpose of her correction was to make her right with God and with the community again. As a member of the community, she had full access to spiritual, emotional, and financial support, necessities for a single mother.

This is the role of the church: to facilitate both individual and group relationships with God and with each other. Often, that process is very delicate. Sometimes that process involves correction, but that correction must always be done in love with the ultimate purpose of the restoration of relationship.

Falling Short of Spiritual Excellence

Many of us don't understand the kind of love that God requires of us, so it's a goal of which we often fall short.

We get it. Church is sometimes frustrating and church people can be annoying, hurtful, and sometimes even evil. Maybe you left your church because it wasn't doing anything in the community, or because some—maybe even a lot of people in the church—are hypocrites. You found out your pastor didn't practice everything he or she preached, or you realized the church is full of judgmental people. Or maybe you no longer wanted to be associated with people who continue to do terrible things in the name of Christianity. Perhaps you think, "If *that's* what a Christian is, then I am not a Christian."

We have both succumbed to this kind of thinking. I, Clarise, ended my relationship with my church some years ago because of this kind of thinking. My young mind couldn't see past the hypocrisy of people's actions, the selfishness of their intentions, the way they used religious beliefs to control others in an attempt to feel powerful, valuable, intimidating, and important. I felt there was a lack of honesty and transparency and it turned me off. And so, I rejected church completely for a while. I stopped going to church altogether, and to be honest, it was liberating. Stepping away allowed me to heal and it gave me the perspective I needed to look at things more objectively and truthfully, but it also revealed that there was a hole in my life that being part of a community of believers was fulfilling. Nothing else could replace that.

It took me years to figure out what was really going on; I didn't like the *culture* of my religion, but I had no issue with the beliefs themselves. In other words, I disagreed with *how* many of the members of my religion practiced the principles they said they believed in and *where* they put their focus. There was a clear disconnect between their actions and the truth they professed. I agreed with the doctrine, but saw all too clearly the selfishness and distortions they'd injected into that doctrine. That made me angry and hurt, and I left the church based on those feelings because I didn't recognize at that time that my value in God makes me more powerful than the distortions that had been revealed to me. What I also didn't know at that time is that the members of my church community didn't have to control me or my community experience the way I had allowed them to.

Once I recognized what the real issue was, with God's guidance, I was able to return to church with a clearer focus: namely, Christ alone. In order to get past the hypocrisy that people still had, I couldn't focus on how that hypocrisy had hurt and traumatized me in the past. I had to wholly focus on the One Who died for all, me included. That doesn't mean the pain of my past church experiences went away; I was and am still processing them. But what it does mean is that when I'm faced with similar people and situations now, I recognize the situation for what it is. I know what's really going on, and with that knowledge it's easier for me to shake my head at foolishness and move on, making sure I'm focused on the right Person. Only through Him can I worship with people with whom I am still rebuilding community.

I, Paul, had a similar experience. In my early 20s I grew disillusioned with my church and I intentionally went on what I call a "church search." I visited other denominations, some Christian and some not, in search of a better way forward with God. I was looking for a better vehicle to get me to the same destination: an authentic relationship with God. Like my sister, I never lost belief in God or in Jesus. But I had a real problem with a lot of the people who were claiming to represent Him. It was the culture of my religion that I struggled with; if I'm honest, I sometimes still struggle with the culture of my religion. I never had a problem with the ideals or the principles for which it stood, even at times when I had a serious problem with the people who claimed to believe the same things that I believed.

If Jesus is the head of the church,[2] what should our response be when church people mismanage their responsibility? Does it make sense to say "I believe in God, but I don't believe in church"? No, it doesn't make sense if you truly understand what church is supposed to be. The problem is, many of us don't understand.

What Church Is

The church is a community of believers headed by Christ.[3] The church is not a building, one religion or even a particular set of religious practices; it's a group of people who believe in, love, and live by Jesus's example. When Jesus talks about the

---

[2] Ephesians 5:23; Colossians 1:17-18; Hebrews 10:19-21
[3] John 15:5 (NIV) - "I am the vine; you are the branches. If you remain in me and I in you, you will bear much fruit; apart from me you can do nothing."

vine and the branches in John 15, He is speaking to the disciples. We may have a tendency to hear this text individually, but Jesus was talking to a *group* of followers. The "you" in the text can represent the church, but it can't logically represent one person apart from the group, based on its context. A branch cannot be a branch unless it is part of the vine.

Also known as "The Body of Christ," the church is supposed to function in the world the way Jesus did while He was here. It is the church's job to reveal and mirror Christ by taking care of the less fortunate, caring for the marginalized, and fighting for those who cannot fight for themselves.[4] Believers are all called to follow the same principle, but the way different people live out that principle shouldn't be cookie-cutter. There are a lot of different ways to be marginalized, and a lot of different ways to help those who are marginalized.

For example, there is an interfaith community in Maryland called Action in Montgomery (AIM). "AIM believes in the ability of people to take leadership and transform their communities. AIM is committed to training and developing neighborhood leaders so that they can change the economic and social structures that affect their lives."[5] AIM recently intervened when an elementary school in their county, a school primarily made up of minorities, was not being given appropriate resources from the district, despite the fact that their school building was in a state of severe disrepair. Meanwhile, other schools in the county, schools that were not on the county's priority list for repairs, received significant funding for building upgrades.

---

[4] Micah 6:8; James 1:27
[5] https://actioninmontgomery.org/about/

AIM's member churches started a campaign of calling, emailing, and writing letters to the school board about the minority school and the resources it needed. After several months of consistent communication, the district reversed a previous decision to delay building a new school for these students and instead voted to move forward with those plans immediately.

One of the loudest voices in this instance came from a pastor whose church is not affiliated with the school, and whose young son is not enrolled there.[6] This was not an act of church people looking out for themselves; this was an act of pure, other-centered altruism. It's the church looking out into the community and working to meet a specific need with no expectation of repayment.

The church is like a rescue vessel on a stormy sea. The ship searches the watery terrain, looking for people in distress who need their support. When they find someone who needs help, they marshal their own resources to fight against the rolling tide on behalf of the endangered. Through this, they demonstrate the character of Jesus Christ, who said in Mark 10:45, "For even the Son of Man did not come to be served, but to serve, and to give his life as a ransom for many." God's intention is for His vehicles to save

> "The church is like a rescue vessel on a stormy sea."

---

[6]Shahzad, Maryam. "Organizers Urge Council to Prioritize South Lake Elementary School." *Montgomery Community Media*, 2 Oct. 2020, www.mymcmedia.org/organizers-urge-council-to-prioritize-south-lake-elementary-school/.

the community rather than keep the occupants of those vehicles as comfortable as possible.

What Church Isn't

Of course, whenever there are people around, there's also sin around, so the Body of Christ often doesn't follow the example of Jesus. Thus, church is *not* a group of perfect people who have no flaws and make no mistakes. Flaws and mistakes can be quite costly, however. It can look like leadership taking advantage of God's people; racism, sexism, or any other "ism"; maintaining the status quo when the status quo hasn't been effective for decades; neglecting or harming the community around them or even some of its own members; running like a country club where only certain people are allowed in and others are kept out, or any number of other church infractions and cruelties.

All of these violations have huge potential to hurt a church's individual members and the community around the church in very deep and long-lasting ways and, therefore, to damage the image of God. When members of the church harm other members of the church, it's self-mutilation. Some people's most traumatic experiences happened in their home churches surrounded by their church community and done by those who profess the love of Jesus over their lives.

When a church is operating outside God's will, people tend to leave as a natural consequence because they no longer feel a spiritual connection at church or within their religious community. It's easy to go to church just because that's what you've always done, and it can become a tradition rather than a relationship with God and His community. The church is not simply a list of regulations or going through the motions because that's what you're used to doing. In fact, God hates that type of "worship."

In Isaiah 1, God speaks to Isaiah in a vision regarding the condition of Israel (the church of that time). In verse 10, God says, "Hear the word of the Lord, you rulers of Sodom; listen to the instruction of our God, you people of Gomorrah!" There's a clear identity crisis here. Israel is supposed to be God's chosen people, but they've forgotten who they are, and God then calls them out as Sodom and Gomorrah.[7]

For the next several verses, God disciplines Israel and gives them a pretty brutal lecture, going so far as to say Israel's offerings are meaningless and their incense is detestable to Him.[8] Isaiah 1:13-14 (NIV) says "I cannot bear your worthless assemblies. Your New Moon feasts and your appointed festivals I hate with all my being." He hates their festivals because they've become robotic, lacking any true significance, which is far from the original intention. He calls their assemblies meaningless because the people are merely "playing the game of church" without building a real relationship with God who will transform their lives and the lives of those around them.

Jesus gave a strong warning about this in Matthew 23:2-3 (NIV):

---

[7] See Genesis 18 & 19 for the full story of Sodom and Gomorrah.
[8] Isaiah 1:13 (NIV): "Stop bringing meaningless offerings! Your incense is detestable to me. New Moons, Sabbaths and convocations—I cannot bear your worthless assemblies."

> The teachers of the law and the Pharisees sit in Moses' seat. So you must be careful to do everything they tell you. But do not do what they do, for they do not practice what they preach. They tie up heavy, cumbersome loads and put them on other people's shoulders, but they themselves are not willing to lift a finger to move them.

It's no wonder people leave the church. Even though the church has potential to be a safe, loving place, it is actually a very dangerous place when it is Spiritless.

Church is also not there for its own good. It is not the church's job to maintain itself. This is not to say that a church shouldn't perform maintenance on the building or pay its bills, but when a church body places the majority of its emphasis on itself, that church body is off mission. The Christian Church is not supposed to be *inward* focused, it is supposed to be *outward* focused. It is not supposed to be *self*-centered, it is supposed to be *other* centered.[9] This is another countercultural idea set forth by Jesus. And by the way, that's exactly what Jesus was doing while He was on Earth: He was creating a *new* culture by which His followers would live—a *Christian* culture.

This distorted culture is what turned us both off from church. We had to step away to gain the perspective we needed to see that the culture of our religion had *become* the religion. We needed to understand that the church will never be what it's meant to be if the people, us included, who understand what church *should* be keep leaving. We had to rededicate ourselves to

---
[9] Acts 2:42-47; Acts 4:32-37

the Biblical meaning of church as we continued to reject the man-inspired, and therefore distorted, meaning of church.

Spiritual Dialysis

The traditional Western worldview tends toward individualism. In the West, we place a higher value on ourselves than we do others around us. We say things like, "Only God can judge me," and "You don't know what I got." We celebrate people who are "self-made" and who "pull themselves up by their bootstraps." English poet William Ernest Henley captures this attitude appropriately in the final stanza of his poem *Invictus:*

> It matters not how strait the gate,
> How charged with punishments the scroll,
> I am the master of my fate,
> I am the captain of my soul.

We aren't saying that taking care of yourself and being inventive during your life's journey are bad virtues. However, those virtues can easily turn into a "me first" attitude when Christ is not at the center of a person's life. "Me first" does not fit into the community that Jesus created, the community that bears His name. Again, Christianity is not *self*-centered, it is *other*-centered. Christians are called to follow the example of Jesus Christ, and His entire life was an example of this attitude: you first (through the power and guidance of God), me second (see "The Essence of God").

Spiritual Dialysis

How, then, should Christians make decisions? If we are not led by our own desires, by what are we led?

In one of his very first books, *The Spiritual Man*,[10] prolific Christian author Watchman Nee discusses a hierarchy through

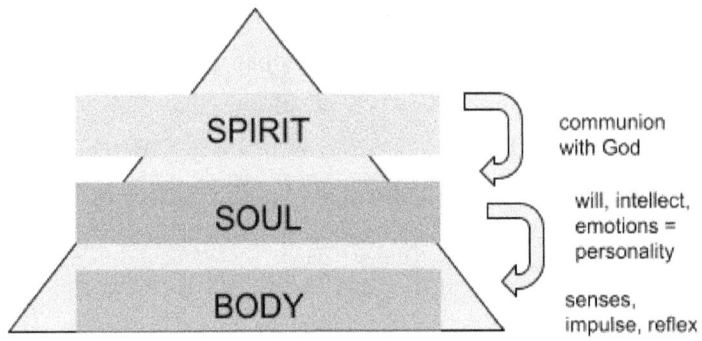

Graphic A: image created by Paul and Clarise Nixon

which he explains the human experience. He describes 3 elements that make up the human being: spirit, soul, and body. Using 1 Thessalonians 5:23[11] as his anchor text, he explains that the spirit is where we have communion with God; the soul is where our will, intellect and emotions are housed; and the body is where we physically experience the world around us through our senses, impulses, and reflexes (Graphic A).

We experience God through our spirit, which communicates through the soul to the body. The soul, then, serves as the medium through which the body is able to experience God in an intimate way. Nee's argument is that this is the original plan of God.

---

[10] Nee, Watchman. "Spirit, Soul and Body." *The Spiritual Man*. Christian Fellowship Publishers, 1977, pp. 21–30.
[11] 1 Thessalonians 5:23 (NIV) - "May God Himself, the God of peace, sanctify you through and through. May your whole spirit, soul and body be kept blameless at the coming of our Lord Jesus Christ."

When sin was introduced, that hierarchy was inverted and the body became the priority over soul and spirit (see Graphic B). In effect, sin introduced the distortion that we are equal with

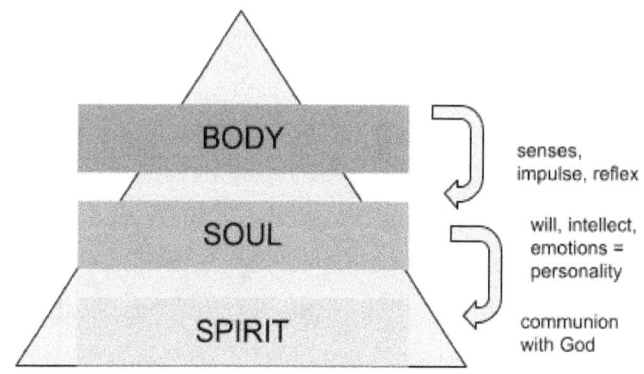

Graphic B: image created by Paul and Clarise Nixon

the animals—creatures who act on impulse and reflex—when in fact we were created to be above the animals and to have dominion over them.[12] Indeed, human beings have the same faculties as animals, such as impulse and instinct, but human beings were not created to rely primarily on those faculties. In humans, bodily faculties are meant to be subject to the intellect, emotions, and will found in the soul, and the soul is intended to be subject to the direction of God as that direction is revealed to man's spirit. Instinct is an important part of the human experience, but to live with instinct as the guiding light of a person's life is limiting to the plan God has for us. We are not mere animals; we are intelligent, willful beings made in the image of God.

---

[12] Genesis 1:28b (NLT) - "...Reign over the fish in the sea, the birds in the sky, and all the animals that scurry along the ground."

But it's important to understand that God's way is counterintuitive to what we know and understand. Self-centeredness is embedded in the fabric of Western society, and it has been since its inception. Our media, whether it's the news, television, movies, or music, have at their core a rigid sense of "me over everyone." Cancel culture is a great illustration of this attitude.

Cancel culture leaves no room for redemption or making any kind of mistake ever when someone has been offended or deeply hurt. In fact, sometimes cancel culture reaches far into a person's past to find wrongdoing with no intention of restoring the relationship, but rather with the intention of utterly destroying a person.

Christian relationships, however, require accountability but also forgiveness and a path forward, both of which are acts of love. For the Christian, "right" can't only be based on our emotions, however justified that might feel. "Right" is based on the Spirit and returning to the original plan for relationships with God and one another.[13]

To adjust our thinking and our living in this way is akin to going through dialysis; our blood—which flows through our entire body and affects everything we think, feel and do—is infected. To heal, we need God to purify every ounce of our blood, our life flow, so that we can live the kinds of lives God intended for us.

---

[13] John 13:35; 17:20-26

The Church Community

We come from a family of ministers. We have close relationships with many professional ministers, including our father, our brother, a few of our uncles and cousins, and many of our parents' friends and our own close friends. Because of our close relationships with professional ministers, we have been witnesses to both great expressions of faith in God, and terrible sins from men and women of God. We have seen up close when things have gone wrong, even within the "safe" confines of the church.

We also realize that, ideally, within a community of believers is the best place to struggle. Being surrounded by other believers who have difficulties and cherished secret sins, and wrestling together in an emotionally and spiritually safe space is God's intention. But in order for iron to sharpen iron,[14] both elements have to be in community with one another and God. This requires massive amounts of vulnerability and trust, however, which are the pinnacles of long-lasting, authentic relationships.

The Church should take outsiders and invite them to become insiders with Jesus so they can grow together into a dwelling place for God.[15] Bible-believing Christians, then, have a responsibility to be pro-church *and* pro-God; these ideas are meant to be one in the same. Hebrews 10:24-25 (ESV) says, "And let us consider how to stir up one another to love and good works, not neglecting to meet together, as is the habit of

---

[14] Proverbs 27:17 (NIV) - "As iron sharpens iron, so one person sharpens another."
[15] Ephesians 2:19-22

some, but encouraging one another, and all the more as you see the Day drawing near."

When Church Isn't Church

Some may say, "But the church isn't doing its job."

In some cases, that's absolutely true, and it's a fair criticism. Some churches are not doing their jobs the way the Bible describes. Some churches are inward-focused and have no real presence in the community. Some churches seem to operate like exclusive VIP clubs that punish and shame members whose sins become public. Some churches even reject certain members because of what they look like, what they can or cannot offer to the church, or for other un-Christlike reasons.

What is the appropriate response in these situations? Is God ok if we leave for reasons like these?

We believe the answers to these questions are too nuanced for us to answer. We believe that God has specific instructions for each of us, and those instructions might differ dramatically from one person to the next. For one, God might want you to remain in the toxic church community in order to affect change or for some other reason. For another reason, God might want you to take a short break from the church community to refresh yourself in Him, then to return to the church community with revived perspective and energy. For yet another reason, God might want you to behave as Paul and Barnabas in Acts 13: to shake the dust off your feet and move on to a new community.[16] Or God might want you to do something else altogether.

Whatever God's specific instructions are for you regarding your situation, we are convinced that, even if the solution is to leave your specific church community, God is not asking you to leave the entire believing community. You might be called to leave your church, your city, your state, your country, or even your denomination, but you are not called to leave *Him* or to permanently disconnect from His larger community.

It can take many different forms and look many different ways, but God wants us to be intimately connected to Him through Jesus and also intimately connected to one another.

---

[16] Acts 13: 51 (NIV) - "So they shook the dust off their feet as a warning to them and went to Iconium."

Practical Steps for Spiritual Dialysis

1. Pray about how you can regain or create love for a community that has hurt, ignored, or neglected you.

2. Study Isaiah 1:1-17. From these verses, write a list of offenses the church in Isaiah's day did wrong and God's intention for the church. Compare this list to your own church life. What are specific areas of your church life upon which you can improve?

3. If your church is distorting the image of God through its practices, fight for it instead of leaving. Because the church is the body of Christ, the reputation of the church and, therefore, Christ's reputation, is on the line. You don't always have to reinvent the wheel; just join the fight by finding and joining an existing community organization in your area that is doing necessary work and add your passion to their cause.

4. Journal Prompt - Make 2 lists: one that focuses on explicit reasons why you want to leave (or have already left) your church (e.g., the pain/trauma you experienced) and another list that focuses on what God is revealing through the Bible and communion with Him about your situation. What are God's specific instructions to you? Study the following passages/characters as you search for answers:

- Is God permitting you to leave? Read Acts 15, which highlights a situation that leads fellow believers to "agree to disagree" and part ways while still continuing their spiritual journeys.

5. Is God allowing you to take a short break? During Jesus' ministry, He often left the toxic environment around Him to refresh Himself, but always came back to the community to continue His mission.

   - Luke 22:39-44 - Jesus prays on the Mount of Olives
   - Luke 5:16 - Jesus withdraws to pray
   - Matthew 14:1-13 - Jesus withdraws to grieve
   - Mark 6:30-32 - Jesus leads the disciples to rest after their ministry tour

6. Is God requiring you to stay where you are?

   - Hosea 1-3 - Hosea called to marry a prostitute
   - Jeremiah 20 - Jeremiah in prison

7. Is God asking you to go somewhere you don't want to go?

   - Exodus 3 - God's call to Moses
   - Jonah 1-3 - Jonah called to Nineveh

Spiritual Dialysis

COMPREHENSION QUESTIONS BASED ON THE CHAPTER

1. What is the rhetorical situation (communicator, audience, and message) of the chapter, and why does this context matter?
2. What is the stated or implied thesis statement of the chapter?
3. How do the authors define spiritual excellence?
4. Explain what the authors say is the purpose of church.
5. Explain what the authors believe church should *not* be.
6. According to Watchman Nee, how has the hierarchy of the human experience been distorted over time?
7. Why do the authors argue that bible-believing Christians should be both pro-church and pro-God?

Writing Questions
1. Think of a time when a church organization did not meet its obligation *according to the Biblical standard as outlined in this chapter*. In what way(s) did they fail to meet their obligations? What should they have done differently?
2. Identify one or two small things you can do outside of or separate from a larger organization (such as a church or a community service organization) to help your immediate community. How can you be a small "church" unto yourself with your actions in the community?
3. Explore how Jesus created a new culture on Earth with the way He lived His life. What are the main goals of this new culture, and by what methods are these goals achieved?

4. Find an organization (similar to AIM) that actively provides an example of what the church is supposed to do. What are their goals and how do they achieve them? How do you know their work is effective?
5. Read and annotate Isaiah 1 (using the Logic Of if necessary). Golden Rule: every underline/highlight needs a corresponding comment.

It's God's Prerogative

God is a supreme Person. God has the right to override His own laws because God is sovereign.

Isaiah 55:8-9 (NIV)
"For my thoughts are not your thoughts, neither are your ways my ways, declares the Lord. As the heavens are higher than the earth, so are my ways higher than your ways and my thoughts than your thoughts."

God created a world that operates according to natural laws. There is a rhythmic *cause and effect* process that takes place in our world, and this process allows us to interact with the natural world. If you till the soil and plant and water seeds during the proper season, the natural result is the growth of crops. If you drop an egg out of the window, the natural result is that it will fall to the ground and break. If you apply sufficient heat to a pot of water, the natural result is that the water will boil and eventually evaporate. We know and understand these natural laws and use them to help us navigate our lives.

There are also supernatural laws. These are laws that are not predictable, that are not bound by science or nature or logic, and that transcend even human understanding. God is the only one who controls these supernatural laws, and when He does so to our perceived benefit, we call it *mercy* or *grace*. The New Oxford American Dictionary defines mercy as "compassion or forgiveness shown toward someone whom it is within one's power to punish or harm." When God doesn't dole out the punishment you rightly deserve, that is an act of mercy.

The same dictionary defines grace as "the free and unmerited favor of God, as manifested in the salvation of sinners and the bestowal of blessings." When God gives you blessings that you don't deserve, that is an act of grace. When and how He chooses to give grace and mercy are completely up to Him because God is in charge. God is sovereign, meaning God possesses supreme and ultimate power over the entire universe,[1] including the natural laws He created for us, and the supernatural laws that only He controls.

How God exercises His sovereignty can really be difficult to grasp emotionally and intellectually because we are created beings. God can choose to give mercy and grace however He wants, and the way He makes those choices doesn't always make sense to us.[2] As created beings, we have a limit to what we can fully understand. More fully understanding God, then, requires intellectual humility on our part: we have to be conscious of the limits in our own knowledge.[3] This intellectual disposition sets

> "God can choose to give mercy and grace however He wants, and the way He makes those choices doesn't always make sense to us."

---

[1] New Oxford American Dictionary - definition of *sovereign*
[2] Isaiah 55:8-9 (NIV) - "For my thoughts are not your thoughts, neither are you ways my ways," declares the Lord. "As the heavens are higher than the earth, so are my ways higher than your ways and my thoughts higher than your thoughts."
[3] Paul, Richard, and Linda Elder. "Essential Intellectual Traits." *The Miniature Guide to Critical Thinking: Concepts and Tools*. Rowman & Littlefield, 2020, p. 24.

the stage for us to increase our faith in the One who has no such limitation; our limitation is an opportunity to grow closer to God.

God is Sovereign

God has the right to override His own laws. So even though God has set up systems in the world—systems such as gravity, gestation, vibration, cause and effect, and others—He retains the right to operate for us outside of these systems within His infinite capacity for mercy and grace. Dr. John S. Nixon Sr. says it this way:

> But since God is not limited to His creation, science and reason cannot disclose all that He wants us to know about Him. That is why, in all of the things of God, faith must have priority as 'the evidence of things not seen' (Hebrews 11:1). Then faith's reasonableness becomes clear—but only to the one who first believes (John 7:17).[4]

In the Christian world, we have fragments of understanding about this idea of supernatural laws and how they work. For example, if the end of the month is coming and we are short on rent money, we might pray for God's grace in that situation. We might ask God to bless us with money we didn't earn and don't deserve so that we can pay the rent. In this way, we are praying for God's grace to override the natural law of cause and effect:

---

[4] Nixon, John S. *Redemption in Genesis: the Crossroads of Faith and Reason.* p. 13

we didn't work, but we want compensation so we can meet our needs. Or we might pray for God's mercy when we are caught doing something we know we shouldn't do. We know we should be punished, but we pray for mercy so that we don't have to endure the embarrassment and pain that we rightly deserve.

Our vision tends to be limited to what we think is good for us. Some of us are quick to pray for God to rescue us from a bad situation that we created for ourselves, but how often do we pray for God to use the bad situation that we're in to bring us closer to Him? We often tend to pray for our own comfort, which may or may not be part of God's will for us. Sometimes, God doesn't rescue us from the situations we created for ourselves because He wants to use them to build intimacy with us.

As educators, we both have a great deal of experience with the ideas of grace and mercy. In fact, "grace" and "mercy" are, historically speaking, two of our students' favorite words. Typically, the terms are used as code for "give me what I want, whether I deserve it or not." Students don't come to us asking for grace when what they want is the natural result of the course they are already on. Our students have used "grace" and "mercy" as a way to reverse the natural cause and effect course that they have already started.

One particular semester I, Paul, had a student who wanted to join my class after the enrollment deadline. She emailed me asking for, you guessed it, "grace and mercy" that I would allow her to enroll in the class. I was struck by her use of the all too familiar terms, and I responded to her request by addressing her usage. Below is a portion of my reply:

> Because this class is a 6-week intensive, it's not necessarily an act of grace or mercy to allow you to join it more than a week late. There is already a lot of work to do in a very short period of time, and if you joined now there would not be less work, only less time. So, before I give you permission to join, you and I must both be certain that you can be successful in the course.

The student's idea of grace was limited to getting what she wanted. As the professor, though, I had a much clearer idea of what would be required for her to learn the skill in the context of the class, and I responded to her request with a much fuller knowledge than she possessed. I did allow this student to enter the class, but only after she and I agreed on specific terms of her enrollment.

Similarly, I, Clarise, was quite flexible with assignment deadlines during the Fall 2020 semester, the first full semester entirely during COVID-19. Because I knew students were dealing with everyday stresses, learning college culture, experiencing homesickness, adjusting to new COVID-19 protocols *and* dealing with a pandemic, I was much more conscious of their mental health and how it was affecting their ability to meet deadlines. As an educator, I know that giving students more time does not necessarily lead to better quality work. More often, it leads to more procrastination on the students' parts. However, because I sensed that many of my students' mental health was in severe danger, I prioritized the instant gratification I knew they'd feel when I extended a deadline for them rather than prioritizing the quality of work they'd give me.

After the semester was complete and I was reflecting on the decisions I'd made, I realized that even though I had good intentions, I had not given them grace. Extending the deadline only prolonged the stress they felt about certain assignments, which increased their anxiety and was the exact opposite of what I'd intended for them. In the moment, though, I rationalized incorrectly that I was being gracious; I focused on their short-term relief rather than their long-term learning. It would have been much more helpful if I'd provided resources to help them process their emotions *while* meeting deadlines for their classes.

Whether we are giving or receiving grace, our understanding of the phenomenon is limited because we are limited beings. And often, we want to manipulate God's sovereignty for our own gain and for no other reason. But God is the unlimited, omniscient Sovereign of the whole Universe. His understanding is not limited, and He always operates for our ultimate good, even if we never recognize it (see "The Essence of God").

The fact is that God rarely overrides His natural laws. As Sovereign, God can override any laws that He wants. But He usually allows those natural laws to operate in the way He intended them. When He does choose to override natural law, we call it a *miracle*. A miracle is "a surprising and welcome event that is not explicable by natural or scientific laws and is therefore considered to be the work of a divine agency."[5]

---

[5] New Oxford American Dictionary

Miracles certainly do happen, but God does not *always* perform the miracles we're praying for. And in these instances, we, the authors, believe God is still being gracious.

In other words, sometimes God tells us no. And, as Sovereign, He is completely within His rights to do so.

God Uses Our Circumstances

If we are going to truly build and nurture a relationship with God, we must come to a critical understanding: God's priority is not necessarily our priority. As human beings, we tend to prioritize things we can

> "...sometimes God tells us no. And, as Sovereign, He is completely within His rights to do so."

feel and that gratify us, things like comfort and safety, experiencing pleasure and avoiding pain. None of these things are evil or even negative in and of themselves, and we, the authors, are not suggesting that people should *embrace* pain or *avoid* pleasure. But what people must realize is that God is not *most* concerned with our comfort. God wants us to experience His joy, and He wants us to have fun in Him (see "Eden Is A Playground"); but that isn't His greatest desire for us. When our comfort stands in the way of God's grand purpose, then God is willing to sacrifice our short-term comfort for the greater goal.

God's grand purpose is reconciling humanity to a full, unfiltered, intimate relationship with Him. While it is possible, and to us perhaps even preferable, that God's purpose will mean we get to be rich and famous, the absence of that lifestyle does not negate God's greater purpose. God can use your comfort for the greater good, but He doesn't have to. In fact, God is willing to ruin your plans (from your point of view) if it means saving your soul.

You might argue against the idea of God ruining your plans using Biblical proof to support your position. You might say, "But what about Romans 8:28: 'All things work together for the good of those who love him.' Doesn't that mean me?" Yes, it does, but that doesn't necessarily mean what you might think it means. "Together for the *good*" means your ultimate good, not necessarily your immediate comfort. God is interested in your salvation, whether your circumstances are good or bad, pleasurable or painful.

Consider these Biblical Examples

70 Years of Captivity

Israel had been consistently disobeying God, so in Jeremiah 25, God told Israel that He would empower King Nebuchadnezzar of Babylon, enemies of God's chosen nation Israel, to overthrow the Israelites. It doesn't say that God would *allow* Nebuchadnezzar to win the war; it says that God would *call* Nebuchadnezzar, *His servant*, to do this work on God's behalf (NIV). God used the enemy of His people to defeat His people in war, and it was not an act of abandonment; it was an act of love. The text says that Israel would be captive to Babylon for 70 years, and that after 70 years God would punish Babylon and free Israel.[6]

---

[6] Jeremiah 25:8-14

If we think about it from the perspective of the individual Israelites, it's kind of a confusing story. If it's true that all things work together for my individual good, as Romans 8:28 might appear to say, then how was decades of Babylonian captivity for the *good* of the people? Certainly some Israelites fasted and prayed for their deliverance during those 70 years, which is a *lifetime* of praying and fasting without getting the results you're praying for. The Bible records that God freed Israel after 70 years, and not before.[7] During the 70 years of captivity, there were people who were born into slavery and who died in slavery; those people had nothing to do with the original reason God punished the Israelites, yet their entire lives were lived in captivity.

The Deadly Census

We see a similar situation in 2 Samuel 24. The Bible says God *incited* David to take a census because God was angry with the Israelites, and He used David to punish the nation. As a result of David taking the census, God killed 70,000 Israelites with a plague. How many of those 70,000 had nothing to do with the original reason God was angry? It's possible that not all 70,000 were guilty, yet all 70,000 experienced the wrath of God. In addition, the families and friends of the 70,000 who died continued to feel God's wrath through the grief of losing their loved ones.

In both of these biblical stories, and many other stories throughout the Bible, God is sovereign.

---

[7] Jeremiah ch. 40

Again, God has a higher purpose for our lives than we typically have for ourselves because He's working for our salvation. His desire is for our relationship to return to the fullness of what He originally intended before sin. Before Eve even bit the forbidden fruit, God had already started working on our behalf,[8] and He hasn't stopped working since then. From Genesis to Revelation, the Bible tells one long story about God guiding His people *back* into communion with Himself. And the story is still being written even now.

Lessons from Job

Perhaps the finest Biblical example of complete trust in God's sovereignty is found in the book of Job. The Bible says that Job is a God-fearing man who is the greatest man in the East; he shuns evil, he has a huge family and he is crazy rich. God suggests that Satan try to get Job to turn against God by taking everything Job has and only sparing Job's life. Satan obliges and kills Job's entire family, except his wife, he kills all of Job's servants and animals, and he ruins all his crops. Job responds by mourning his losses and *praising God* for God's sovereignty.[9]

Later, Job asks God why God has targeted him,[10] using Job's deeds as evidence of his righteousness. Job says that he doesn't deserve how he's being treated, and here's the key: he's right. He doesn't deserve it. Yet, Job isn't being *mistreated*. How

---

[8] 1 Peter 1:20 (NIV) - He was chosen before the creation of the world, but was revealed in these last times for your sake.
[9] Job 1
[10] Job 7:20 (NLT) - "If I have sinned, what have I done to you, O watcher of all humanity? Why make me your target? Am I a burden to you?"

It's God's Prerogative

is that possible? It's a simple answer: God is sovereign. His purpose is beyond ours, and He does not have to answer to us.

From the reader's perspective, we see more fully the context of Job's situation than even Job did himself. Because we have the entire Bible, we know that God's ultimate purpose in the circumstances of Job's life is to prove to Satan that Job respects and loves the Lord and trusts in His ultimate sovereignty.[11] It's problematic when we try to evaluate something that is beyond us based on our context and understanding. This is re-making God in our image, another form of egocentricity.

God's sovereignty means He isn't subject to our evaluation at all. God reminds Job of this in verses 7 and 8 of chapter 40 (NLT): "Brace yourself like a man; I will question you, and you shall answer me. Would you discredit my justice? Would you condemn me to justify yourself?" When Job asks God (quite respectfully) why he is going through what he is going through, God responds with 4 chapters of sarcasm.[12] He tells Job to be quiet and not question Him.

Job 38-41 are some of our favorite chapters in the Bible because of the level of sarcasm that seeps from the rhetorical questions God asks Job in response to Job's question. Here are a couple of our favorites:

- God asks Job if Job is in charge of the dawn in Job 38:12-13 (NLT): "Have you ever commanded the morning to appear and caused the dawn to rise in the

---

[11] Job 1:8-12
[12] Job chs. 38-41

east? Have you made daylight spread to the ends of the earth, to bring an end to the night's wickedness?"

- God asks Job for directions to light and darkness in Job 38:19-21 (NLT): "Where does light come from, and where does darkness go? Can you take each to its home? Do you know how to get there? But of course you know all this! For you were born before it was all created, and you are so very experienced!"

God spends all of chapter 41 asking Job if Job can tame a Leviathan.[13] Here are verses 1-3 (NIV) from that chapter: "Can you pull in Leviathan with a fishhook or tie down its tongue with a rope? Can you put a cord through its nose or pierce its jaw with a hook? Will it keep begging you for mercy? Will it speak to you with gentle words?"

Job clearly does not have the answer to any of these questions, and that's God's point entirely. He's saying to Job, "I am God and I am sovereign. Trust Me."

So not only does Job suffer, he also never gets real answers to his questions; he never understands *why* he suffers the way he does, but he always trusts in God's sovereignty.[14] As it relates to trusting in God's sovereignty, Job 13:15a (KJV) might be the most powerful verse in the Bible: "Though He slay me, yet will I trust in Him."

Not only that, Job says in Job 42:5, "My ears had heard of You, but now my eyes have seen You." Job recognizes that his

---

[13] *Encyclopedia Britannica* describes a leviathan as a sea monster in Jewish culture. It appears in the following books of the Bible: Psalms, Job, Isaiah and Amos.
[14] Job 42:1-6

relationship with God has become a more personal relationship through his suffering, and because God responded to Him. Again, God's ultimate goal is to bring us into a fuller relationship with Himself, and sometimes that's done through severe suffering and testing, as it was in Job's case.

The *only* reason Job went through the terrible hardships that he did was because God was proving a point; He was defending His reputation to Satan. And He's still defending His reputation now to the whole universe. This means that sometimes God's methods are beyond our understanding. Sometimes we will never know in our lifetime why we go through what we have to go through. It means that sometimes God will not rescue us from our situation.

COVID-19 is a more recent example of God's sovereignty. We had nothing to do with the onset of the virus, yet many of us are suffering greatly and losing close friends and relatives because of it, even if those friends and relatives followed all of the protocols. In these circumstances, God is still sovereign.

God's Sovereignty in Our Lives

Understanding God's sovereignty using Bible stories is necessary, but in order to come to a full understanding of the kind of person God is, you need to experience Him for yourself.

God's Sovereignty in My Career

I, Clarise, had a very difficult time finding work in the publishing and technical communication fields after I finished my graduate program. I did what I was supposed to do to look for a job at that time: I thoroughly researched companies, whether they had public job openings or not, printed out a bunch of resumes, put on a suit and "hit the pavement" every single day. I visited countless businesses in multiple states, made phone calls, and even had a lot of really good interviews.

I was finding many job opportunities, but for some reason, nothing was working out. My anxiety levels shot through the roof and my feelings were really starting to be hurt because I *knew* I was qualified for these jobs, and I *knew* I'd be an asset to these companies. I also *knew* I was going about finding a job the "right" way, so it didn't make sense to me that I couldn't get hired.

Then one day, I received a call from the department chair of my undergraduate program at my alma mater. He wanted to know if I was interested in being an adjunct professor in the English department. Being an educator in the traditional sense was something I'd never wanted to do; I just felt the classroom wasn't for me. My entire life, though, I'd heard the refrain over and over from different people, unrelated to each other: "You're going to be a teacher one day." They saw something in me that made it abundantly clear to them what my calling was. Every time I heard them say it, though, I got annoyed because it wasn't what I wanted for myself. Education in the general sense, yes, but not the classroom. So, when I was looking for jobs, I never considered looking for teaching jobs.

But because I was so desperate for work after my graduate program, when I was offered an adjunct position, I didn't have to think about it for very long at all. My focus had changed: it was either move back in with my parents or work with whomever offered me a position. And the one and only job offer I received at that time was to be an adjunct professor.

It's God's Prerogative

So, my career in traditional higher education began. My decision was validated the very first moment I opened my mouth to welcome my very first classroom of students. The moment I spoke—it was something simple like "Good morning"—a massive weight was lifted off of my shoulders that I didn't realize I'd been carrying for years up until that very moment. I felt in my bones that this was what I was meant to be doing.

Over the next several months, I began to reflect on all the jobs I'd had growing up: writing tutor, reading tutor, editor, etc. Each one had a classroom component attached to it. I'd been in teacher training nearly my entire life and had no idea. I also began to reflect on what people had always said to me, and the deep feeling of anger that had started to build in me because I wanted something else for myself. Little did I know at the time that I was having an internal struggle with what I wanted for me and what God had for me.

There's no way I would have accepted that adjunct position if I wasn't in a desperate situation. I know now that I couldn't get hired anywhere else, not because I wasn't qualified, but because I wasn't being obedient to Christ. The world opened up to me the moment I obeyed. But before that, I felt like my life was falling apart and I couldn't understand why I was doing everything right, but the Lord was not opening any doors for me. In God's sovereignty, He knew that in order to break through my stubborn nature, He had to close every single door that I was trying to walk through. It felt terrible at the time, but it was for my ultimate good.

God's Sovereignty in My Near-Death Experience

In 2001, I, Paul, had recently graduated from college and I was involved in a terrible car accident. A group of us had driven together from Alabama to Oklahoma to celebrate our close friends' wedding with them. On the 8-hour drive home my brother, John, fell asleep behind the wheel. It was after 3 a.m., the Arkansas highway was totally empty, and he had the cruise control set at 80 miles per hour. The car careened off of a 30-foot cliff with 4 passengers inside: John was in the driver's seat; his wife of less than a year at that time was in the passenger's seat; I was sitting behind my sister-in-law and my girlfriend at the time was sitting behind my brother.

Everyone in the car was asleep when we went over the cliff.

By the time the car landed, everyone in the car was awake—except me.

John was able to pull his wife and my girlfriend from the destroyed vehicle, but he could not get me out of the car. At my girlfriend's insistence, John climbed up the steep embankment to get help. He flagged down a truck driver who hurried over, saw the catastrophe, and used his CB radio to call for help. I had to be removed from the car with a metal-bending contraption called the Jaws of Life. My injuries were so severe that they had to call in a helicopter to airlift me to the hospital.

When my parents arrived at the hospital several hours later, the doctors still weren't sure if I would survive. "It's touch and go," one doctor told my father.

It's God's Prerogative

Everyone else was injured, but their troubles were not life threatening. John had cracked some ribs; his wife had some bleeding on her brain, a separated right shoulder, and some scarring on her right arm; and my girlfriend had broken her left femur and her left clavicle.

I had gotten the worst of it. I had broken every bone in my face, I had a bruised lung and kidney, I had broken several vertebrae in my back and, worst of all, I had suffered a severe Traumatic Brain Injury (TBI). The doctors couldn't even begin to address my broken bones until the swelling on my brain went down. They weren't sure that the swelling would ever go down, which is why they had given my father such a grim report.

The swelling on my brain did go down, the doctors were able to repair my face, I was able to fully regain my mobility after weeks of physical therapy, and my TBI did not cause permanent damage. Now when I tell people the story of the accident, some are hesitant to believe that I'm telling the truth. I talk about my broken back and they're amazed that I walk so well—without so much as a limp. One of the most common effects of a TBI is trouble with processing language. I have had a successful career of almost 20 years doing exactly that—processing language—as a teacher, professor, writer, and editor, all taking place after I suffered a TBI.

I was in the back seat of the car with my seat belt on, asleep at 3 o'clock in the morning. I was where I was supposed to be, doing what I was supposed to be doing. Yet I was the one who suffered the worst injuries, while my brother, the man behind the wheel, literally walked away. It is not an exaggeration to say that I felt a small piece of what Job might have: why was God targeting me?

It has taken many years of prayer and reflection, but I now see that God's ultimate purpose could not be confined to my comfort. My accident experience has brought me closer to God and made me more dependent on Him than I could have ever been without the experience. In this way, the worst thing that ever happened to me is the best thing that ever happened to me.

In looking back at our experiences, we could easily resent God or the process He put us through if we were to reflect on our pasts a certain way. But when we look through our love glasses, we see God's sovereignty the way it truly is: as a component of His love (*see* "The Essence of God").

What if He Doesn't Rescue You?

In the story of Job, the man himself is rescued. The Bible records that God restores what Job had and gives him an increase.[15] Job is rescued, but his 10 original children are not, and neither are his servants. People literally died so God could prove a point to the devil.

Remember the 70 years of the Israelites' captivity at the hands of the Babylonians? During those 70 years, King Nebuchadnezzar built a giant golden statue of himself to celebrate the fact that he was the strongest king in the world. Three young men from the Israelite captives named Shadrack, Meshach, and Abednego refused to bow down to the golden image and were consequently sentenced to death by fire. In the face of this sentence, they respond boldly to the king in Daniel 3:16b-18 (NIV):

---

[15] Job 42:10 (NIV) - "After Job had prayed for his friends, the Lord restored his fortunes and gave him twice as much as he had before."

> King Nebuchadnezzar, we do not need to defend ourselves before you in this matter. If we are thrown into the blazing furnace, the God we serve is able to deliver us from it, and he will deliver us from Your Majesty's hand. But even if he does not, we want you to know, Your Majesty, that we will not serve your gods or worship the image of gold you have set up.

The response of the three Hebrew boys is similar to Job's response. In the face of mortal danger the Hebrew boys said, God can save us, we believe that God will save us, but even if He doesn't, we still will not sin and we will continue to trust His sovereignty. Job said, even if He kills me, and even though He has taken my children and servants, I will trust His sovereignty anyway.

How different are we from Job and the three Hebrew boys? Is our faith dependent on God rescuing us? What if I, Clarise, had never found a job and had to move back in with my parents? Or what if I, Paul, had never recovered from my injuries? Would we still trust in God's sovereignty? The matter is less about God's sovereignty because He's always sovereign; the matter is more about our faith. God is sovereign, so we are being short-sighted when we allow our faith to waiver during the difficult and painful circumstances of life. In many cases, what happens to and around us is a matter of natural law—very often it's simple cause and effect. But our scope is so limited that we can't see it that way. We know we can't see everything, but still, we hesitate to trust God who we know *can* see everything.

Being omniscient, God knows the beginning from the end.[16] God called Nebuchadnezzar "My servant" almost 30 years before Nebuchadnezzar's conversion experience in Daniel 3. God knew Nebuchadnezzar would surrender His life to Him even before Nebuchadnezzar knew it himself. This is because God is omniscient.

There are many stories of people who trust God in the face of overwhelming odds, personal tragedy, and even death. The victory in these situations is not in God rescuing the individual from the circumstances; the victory is in trusting in God's sovereignty in spite of difficult circumstances.

Many of us aren't willing to fully trust God with our careers, our relationships, and our possessions, much less our lives. We trust God as long as He is doing things for us. Life *from* God is often our perspective, when life *with* God should be our goal (*see* "Ridiculous Prayers"). We pray for God's grace and mercy, but what we are often really praying for is for God to give us what we want. To truly build a relationship with God, we must subjugate our desires and prioritize God's will above our own. We must be willing to endure discomfort and difficulty for the glory of God. When we prioritize God over ourselves, we will fully experience the joy and peace God has for us.

---

[16] Isaiah 46:10 (NLT) - "Only I can tell you the future before it even happens. Everything I plan will come to pass, for I do whatever I wish."

Practical Steps for Understanding God's Sovereignty

1. Journal Prompt: What is your true motivation for following Christ? What if, for example, there were no Heaven? Would you still want to be His follower? Are you primarily following Him because of the relationship or because of the rewards? Reflect on these questions in writing.

2. Do a biblical character study of Jonah (Jonah chs. 1-4), Samson (Judges chs. 13-16), and Daniel (Daniel ch. 9-10) using the following questions as a guide:
   - What was their attitude during their hardships?
   - How does God demonstrate grace in these men's lives?
   - How does God show His sovereignty in these stories?

3. Evaluate and/or reflect on a particularly difficult situation or time in your life. Discuss with a Christian friend how God demonstrated grace and sovereignty during this time.

COMPREHENSION QUESTIONS BASED ON THE CHAPTER

1. What is the rhetorical situation (communicator, audience, and message) of the chapter, and why does this context matter?
2. What is the stated or implied thesis statement of the chapter?
3. How can being intellectually humble help us better understand God?
4. What are the similarities between the negative consequences during the Israelites' 70 years of Babylonian captivity and the census during King David's reign?
5. Explain how God's treatment of Job was not *mistreatment* of Job.

Writing Questions

1. Consider the concept of intellectual humility (see p. 127) as it relates to God's sovereignty. Why is it important for human beings to approach their own understanding of God with a sense of intellectual humility?
2. Think of a time outside of a Bible story when you saw or heard about God displaying His sovereignty in a way that directly helped people. How do you know that God was responsible for that instance? What natural law(s) did God override and how did God's actions in that case benefit the people involved?
3. Why is it important for faith to be the first priority in a Christian person's belief system, even before science and reason?

4. The authors write about how "grace" and "mercy" are often translated to mean "give me what I want, whether I deserve it or not" (see p. 129). If the authors are right, this means that receiving "grace" and "mercy" can lead to a person getting something that is *not* good for them. Think of a time when you or someone you know got something they thought they wanted and didn't deserve, and it turned out to be a negative experience. How could the situation have been better if the person had acted in faith instead of operating based on their personal desires?
5. Analyze how God uses rhetorical questions in Job 38-41 (see pp. 136-137).
6. Read and annotate one of the following chapters of the Bible (using the Logic Of if necessary): Job 38-41 (choose 1 chapter); Jeremiah 25; 2 Samuel 24; Daniel 3. Golden Rule: every underline/highlight needs a corresponding comment.

THE PROTAGONIST PROBLEM

God is an attentive Person. Where we place our attention makes a difference in our lives. Pay attention to the things of God and God will enable you to gradually turn your life around.

Proverbs 4:23 (ERV)
Above all, be careful what you think because your thoughts control your life.

The brain is the powerhouse of the human body. It directly affects our different body parts, our thoughts, and our lives by sending and receiving millions of signals every second to the various parts of the body. Many of our thoughts, though, are unconsciously controlled by what we choose to let into our lives. If what we let in is not connected to Christ, our mental capacity becomes distorted, our focus becomes shorter and shorter, and as a result, our spiritual lives plummet. By intentionally focusing on Christ, we can regain the capacity to have close fellowship with Him, thereby improving all areas of our lives.

The Protagonist Problem

Daenerys Targaryen is one of several protagonists in the story about a fight for the Iron Throne in King's Landing on the continent of Westeros. The character is a fan favorite from

The Protagonist Problem

the popular HBO show *Game of Thrones* based on the epic fantasy book series *A Song of Ice and Fire* by George R.R. Martin. She is introduced as a young girl with no real power or support and no claim to the throne in Westeros.

Through 6 seasons, Daenerys acquires a large, loyal following, an army, devoted subjects, ships, various titles, and everything she needs to conquer Westeros, including three dragons. She survives fires, attempted rapes and assassinations, and recovers from acts of treason and betrayal. She frees thousands of slaves from Slaver's Bay, a powerful geographical region in Essos—the continent East of Westeros—renaming the area Bay of Dragons. She shows kindness to strangers, listens to wise counsel, learns to rule and overcomes seemingly insurmountable odds at every turn. Men fall in love with her, children run to her side, friends feel safe with her, and her dragons obey her every command.

By the time she travels to Westeros to claim her throne, the TV audience is enraptured by her. She begins as a naive little girl, and through trial after trial, grows into an intoxicating woman with the adoration of her viewers growing deeper with every heroic act.

But once she reaches Westeros, a land where no one knows her, her queenly essence starts to decay. If her time in Essos is a success story, her time in Westeros is filled with failures from the moment she steps foot on the continent. But our hearts are so enthralled with her, we continue to root for her even when she makes poor choices. We want so badly for her to win that we defend her bad decisions and excuse her acts of evil.

By the end of the 8-season series, Daenerys' character has shifted. Obsessed with winning, and going against the counsel given her, she burns whole cities to the ground, killing tens of thousands of innocents—the very people she came to save as she had done for so many in Essos.

It's a heartbreaking experience for those who have fallen in love with the character and have watched her triumph on so many occasions with seemingly altruistic motives. She is portrayed as saint-like for the first six seasons, but she slowly turns into a demon in the last two.

Even other characters around her notice the shift. At one point, two of her advisors have a conversation about it:

> Varys: I have served tyrants most of my life; they all talk about destiny.
> Tyrion: She's a girl who walked into a fire with three stones and walked out with three dragons. How could she not believe in destiny?
> Varys: Perhaps that's the problem. Her life has convinced her that she was sent here to save us all.

Her life had convinced many of us, too.

Upon examination, we discover eerie similarities between the development of Daenerys' character and our feelings towards her: she overlooks her principles once she gets close to achieving her destiny; once

> "...we tend to cheer for the main characters in a story, in spite of the morality of their actions, simply because they are the main characters."

we fall in love with her, we overlook our principles and continue to applaud her in spite of her actions.

This is the Protagonist Problem: we tend to cheer for the main characters in a story, in spite of the morality of their actions, simply because they are the main characters. The *protagonist* of a story is defined as the leading character of the story, and the action of a story typically follows the protagonist trying to achieve a particular goal. The *antagonist* is defined as the person or group that opposes the protagonist. So the protagonist of a story does not have to be "the good guy"; in fact, if the protagonist is a villain, then the antagonist could very well be "the good guy." In a case such as this, you might find yourself siding with the force of evil in the story.

The reasons we cheer for the protagonists in a particular story are certainly nuanced, but one undeniable fact is common in each case: because the characters are the main characters, we spend a great deal of time with them. Regardless of their beliefs or actions, our spending so much time with them can lead us to excuse many of their misdeeds and to support whatever they are trying to achieve, in spite of whether or not their aspirations are in line with our personal morals and values.

Increased exposure to a thing expands our ability to tolerate, and eventually our ability to appreciate, that thing. Whether the protagonist is male or female, rich or poor, black or white, educated or ignorant, guilty or innocent, even real or fictional, just being the protagonist makes this person sympathetic and relatable because we spend so much time with the character. Humbert Humbert in *Lolita;* Tyler Durden in *Fight Club;* Tom Ripley in *The Talented Mr. Ripley;* Arthur Fleck aka Joker in *Joker*; Lucifer Morningstar in *Lucifer*. On the

Showtime show *Dexter*, the protagonist is a pathological serial killer who is committed to only murdering evildoers in society. Watching the show, you find yourself *hoping* Dexter gets away with murder and *rooting* for his "Dark Passenger," the inner voice that motivates him to take human life.

Indeed, the human being can get used to anything. In some cases, this increased exposure leads to appreciation, as it does with Daenerys; in other cases, it simply leads us to be less mortified by their misbehavior, as it does with Don Draper on *Mad Men*. In any case, we grow accustomed to things that would have repulsed us, if not for our increased exposure to those things.

Controlling the Mind

Neuroscientist Mario Beauregard co-authored a book with journalist Denyse O'Leary called *The Spiritual Brain: A Neuroscientist's Case for the Existence of the Soul*. In the book, the authors reveal some remarkable information about the distinction between the mind and the brain. They demonstrate that the mind is able to manipulate the brain, both in terms of what the brain thinks, and how the brain is physiologically structured. Recent neuroscience has discovered that neural circuits grow when they receive a lot of traffic, and they either shrink or stay the same when they receive minimal traffic.

The authors compare quantum physicists studying particles to people focusing on ideas. Essentially, they reveal that by focusing on ideas we prevent them from decaying; we give our ideas life and power by giving them attention. Logically, then, one way to eliminate an idea from our minds is to simply ignore it.[1]

Not only that, but the adult human brain is actually very plastic. The classical scientific view of the human brain is that by the time the brain reaches adulthood it is fixed, set, it is what it is. But scientists have learned that the human brain continues to be malleable even into adulthood. Where once we thought that "you can't teach an old dog new tricks," we now realize that, in fact, you can. For example, people can voluntarily control their level of response to sad thoughts, and people with phobias can reorganize their brains so they lose their phobias.[2]

The truly fascinating part of all of this brain research is *how* the adult human brain can be changed. Dr. Beauregard reveals the method: "The amount of traffic our neural circuits receive depends, for the most part, on what we choose to pay attention to. Not only can we make decisions by focusing on one idea rather than another, but we can change the patterns of neurons in our brains by doing so consistently."[3] In other words, how we think today helps shape how we will think tomorrow. By committing conscious effort to a thing, we create in our own brains "a pattern of neural activity that becomes a template for action."[4] And because of the plasticity of our brains, we are always able to create new templates by focusing our attention on a particular thing.

Psychologist and expert on positive neuroplasticity Rick Hanson makes essentially the same claim:

---

[1] Beauregard, Mario, and Denyse O'Leary. *The Spiritual Brain*. HarperOne, 2009, p. 33.
[2] Ibid. p. xiii.
[3] Ibid. p. 33
[4] Ibid. p. 34

It's a two-way street: as your brain changes, your mind changes; and as your mind changes, your brain changes. This means—remarkably—that what you pay attention to, what you think and feel and want, and how you work with your reactions to things all sculpt your brain in multiple ways.[5]

No longer can we think and believe that as adults we *are* while children are still *becoming*. Instead, we must recognize that, even as adults, we are also still *becoming*, and what we are becoming is in large part dependent on what we do with our time and attention. And this is the complexity of The Protagonist Problem: when we spend our time and attention *rooting* for evil characters, we are gradually becoming less appalled—and perhaps more enthralled—by their actions. We become more tolerant of evil the more we observe evil.

And, if we're being honest with ourselves, we like observing evil. Wrongdoing is fun to watch. It's also fun to participate in: no one would sin if it wasn't fun. Movies are more fun when people are killing and dying; TV shows are more entertaining when the characters are vicious and cruel; books are better when they depict individuals who are promiscuous and manipulative. Part of why we gravitate towards these stories and characters is because they're mirrors of our lives and of ourselves.

---

[5]Hanson, Rick. "Introduction - Using Your Brain to Change Your Mind." *Dr. Rick Hanson*, 13 Aug. 2018, www.rickhanson.net/introduction-using-your-brain-to-change-your-mind/.

The Protagonist Problem

We like our fictional characters to do the things we wish we *could* do, and perhaps even justify the things we do. So when Dwayne Wayne interrupts Whitley Gilbert's wedding ceremony in *A Different World* to profess his love and steal her from her soon-to-be husband, we boisterously applaud his actions because we think Dwayne and Whitley belong together, in spite of the pain this act inflicts on multiple people. We enjoy the drama of it all because drama is entertaining when it's happening to someone else.

The Protagonist Problem does not only affect us when we're reading books or watching television. It is the reality of humanity that we grow accustomed to what we repeatedly experience, whether that thing is real or fictional. We grow accustomed, even to terrible things, when we experience them frequently. What's more, we learn from the placebo effect[6] that the human brain does not always distinguish between what is real and what is fictional. Following this logic, it's possible that watching someone get killed on screen can have similar effects on the human psyche as seeing a person get killed in real life.

To illustrate, in May of 2020, I, Paul, was buried in my work and I hadn't seen the news. In a group text thread, several of my friends were talking about their feelings of anger and frustration about the day's events. They were talking about how they didn't know what to say to their young black sons, or how to help them navigate the police brutality and racism of 21st century America.

---

[6] Placebo effect - n. - a beneficial effect produced by a placebo drug or treatment, which cannot be attributed to the properties of the placebo itself, and must therefore be due to the patient's belief in that treatment

I texted: "I'm totally in the dark, been buried in work all day. What horrible news did I miss?"

One friend responded: "Cops killing a black man, the usual."

Another friend added: "Same ol same ol."

We were talking about the murder of George Floyd.

We remain outraged, but we tend to get used to even horrible atrocities when they are repeatedly revisited upon us. We each have protagonists in our lives, based on what we spend the most time with and pay the most attention to.

The question, then, becomes, who are the protagonists in your life? What outside influences affect your thinking and, therefore, your desires? Are you in relationship with God in name only, or do you spend so much time with Him that He's the leading character in the story of your life? Do you see yourself as the protagonist of your own life? If so, what things are you excusing in yourself that you need to let God deal with?

The truth is, if God is your copilot, then your plane is certainly going to crash. If you, or anyone else besides God, are the protagonist of your story, then you will gradually grow less and less concerned with the things of God, until, finally, you find yourself so far away from what you once believed that you will be unrecognizable to yourself.

On the road home from Jerusalem, Mary and Joseph lost sight of Jesus for a short while, and it took them *three days* to find Him again.[7] What's interesting about this story is that the Bible spends no time discussing how Mary and Joseph felt

---

[7] Luke 2:41-46

during those three days, although they must have been terrified. Losing and then looking for your son in a town that isn't your home with no idea where he could be must have made them feel panicked. In fact, they didn't just lose their son; they knew He was the Messiah at this point, so they literally lost *God*. Once they found Him, Jesus questioned them: "Why were you searching for me?" he asked. "Didn't you know I had to be in my Father's house?"[8] Jesus didn't do anything wrong in this story; His parents left and didn't bring Him *with* them.

Straying from God for even a little while will have detrimental effects on our lives. Even a short moment of neglect can lead to a long separation. And not because Jesus has moved, but because we don't know where to find Him anymore. And oftentimes, we only notice He isn't near us because we suddenly want something from Him.

Creating a Solution

The good news is, it's not too late to find Jesus! The human mind is extremely plastic, and it is never too late to build new templates for thoughts and behaviors. The key is to focus your attention on the new thing—the *better* thing, namely God as a person. Be intentional about using your mind to control your brain; pay attention to the things of God, and God will enable you to gradually turn your life around.

One solution to being controlled by negative thoughts and outside influences is to upgrade the quality of our thinking. While our thoughts, desires, and actions are all interrelated, they

---

[8] Luke 2:49 (NIV): "Why were you searching for me?" he asked. "Didn't you know I had to be in my Father's house?"

can *all* be strengthened through our thinking. In fact, our lives are destined to improve just by improving the quality of our thinking.[9] This task is definitely a battle between our humanity and God's divinity. Even when we know better, it's still easy to fall back on old habits.[10] While it is possible to change our thinking and our habits, it is certainly not easy to do. We need help, and fortunately, we have help.

We can start each day by taking complete control of our thoughts and giving them over to Christ. As 2 Corinthians 10:5 (ESV) says, "We destroy arguments and every lofty opinion raised against the knowledge of God, and take every thought captive to obey Christ."

An essential step in this process is posturing your heart before God. Any action you take to improve your thinking will not come to its full maturity without the power of the Holy Spirit, who you should invite into your heart at the beginning of each day. Jonathan Leonardo of the Love Reality Tour[11] does this through going to what he calls his "secret place," a place of minimal distraction where he can completely focus on Christ. For him, it's the shower; for you, it might be a quiet drive in your car, or the closet, or somewhere else where you know your heart and mind will be still.

In his January 2017 sermon, Pastor Craig Groeschel of Life.Church suggests creating a list with Words to Live By that includes biblical passages that affirm what God has already promised. He says, "Your life is moving in the direction of your

---

[9] Paul, Richard, and Linda Elder. *The Miniature Guide to Critical Thinking Concepts and Tools.* Rowman & Littlefield, 2020, p. 9
[10] Matthew 26:41 (NIV): "Watch and pray so that you will not fall into temptation. The spirit is willing, but the flesh is weak."
[11] https://www.lovereality.org/

strongest thoughts," and those thoughts can be changed and restored by internalizing biblical truths. Repeating those biblical truths every day helps jump start the process of renewing your thinking. The Bible contains many statements on this very idea:

- Philippians 4:8 (NLT) says, "And now, dear brothers and sisters, one final thing. Fix your thoughts on what is true, and honorable, and right, and pure, and lovely, and admirable. Think about things that are excellent and worthy of praise."

- Romans 12:2 (NIV) says, "Do not conform to the pattern of this world, but be transformed by the renewing of your mind. Then you will be able to test and approve what God's will is—his good, pleasing and perfect will."

- Colossians 3:2-3 (NIV) says, "Set your minds on things above, not on earthly things. For you died, and your life is now hidden with Christ in God."

- Psalm 73:28 (ESV) says, "But for me it is good to be near God; I have made the Lord God my refuge, that I may tell of all your works."

- Proverbs 4:23 (ERV) says, "Above all, be careful what you think because your thoughts control your life."

Be intentional about inviting Christ into your heart and mind day after day, repeating biblical truths, taking captive every stray thought, and making it obedient to Christ.

Practical Steps for Focusing on God

1. Cultivate stillness and quiet in your life.

   - Make it a point to gather at least a few minutes each day to be still and quiet. Spend those minutes in close, personal fellowship with God.

   - Give God your full attention; be mindful of His presence. Silence your cell phone, turn off the TV, and go to a quiet place.

2. Seek God first every day; speak aloud what He says is true.

   - Make a list of the positive characteristics that God placed in you, and find accompanying Bible verses that build your confidence in those characteristics.

   - Instead of beginning your day by checking social media or the news, begin by reading your list aloud to yourself.

   - Start the day by posturing your heart before God, focusing your mind on biblical truths and making every thought captive to the will of Christ.

3. Reduce your exposure to media, even "good" media.

   - Don't just take media away; replace it with something that will help you on your journey.

- Replace media with prayer, reading the Bible, and/or spiritually-focused journaling for a small portion of each day.

Words to Live By Example

Here is an example of a list of biblical truths that you can speak aloud to refocus and, therefore, renew your mind every day.

"I am named by God, not labeled by man. I will walk in the truth of who God says I am:

- I am a child of God. (Galatians 3:26)
- I am content with Christ alone. (Psalms 73:26)
- I am joyful. I am gentle. I am self-controlled. I am patient. (Galatians 5:22-23)
- I am creative, and I will use my creativity to serve God. (Exodus 35:34-35, Colossians 3:23-24)
- I am courageous & self-disciplined (II Timothy 1:7)
- I am empathetic. (Romans 12:15)
- I am loved. (John 3:16)
- The joy of the Lord is my strength. (Nehemiah 8:10)
- God always provides a way out of temptation, and I will look for, recognize, and take it. (1 Corinthians 10:13)
- He will help me; I only need to ask. (Matthew 7:7)
- God meets my needs. (Philippians 4:19)
- I submit to God and resist the devil. (James 4:7)
- I fight for purity, guarding my eyes and heart from tempting situations. (Romans 8:5-6)
- Nothing can separate me from God. (Romans 8:38-39)

- Sin has no power over me. (Romans 6:14)
- I have authority over the devil and I can resist him through Christ. (Luke 10:19; James 4:7)
- I have the mind of Christ. (1 Corinthians 2:16; Philippians 4:8)
- I am not defined by what I have done. Greater is He that lives in me than he that lives in the world. (1 John 4:4)
- My record has been wiped clean. (Psalm 103:12)
- You are my God who keeps His word. You are faithful throughout all the generations. (Psalm 119:90)"

Follow 3 simple steps for creating your own Words to Live By list here: https://finds.life.church/words/

COMPREHENSION QUESTIONS BASED ON THE CHAPTER

1. What is the rhetorical situation (communicator, audience, and message) of the chapter, and why does this context matter?
2. What is the stated or implied thesis statement of the chapter?
3. What do the authors say is the protagonist problem?
4. Explain the scientific evidence that backs up the authors' claim that "no longer can we think and believe that as adults we *are* while children are still *becoming*. Instead, we must recognize that, even as adults, we are also still *becoming*..." (155).
5. What lesson can we learn from the story about Mary and Joseph losing sight of their son, Jesus?

Writing Questions

1. Remember a fictional character from film or television who you rooted for even though the character was evil. What was it about the character that was appealing? Which of your personal morals did you have to overlook in order to be on the character's side? How would you react to this character if they were a person in real life? How would society treat this person in real life?
2. Consider the differences between the mind and the brain (see pp. 154-155). How can you use your mind to control your brain? In what area(s) of your own life could you use your mind to improve your quality of life?

3. The authors refer to research that indicates that "the adult human brain is actually very plastic" (p. 154). Explore how this view of the development of the human brain can affect a person's actions, goals, and outlook.
4. Consider the idea that observing evil can make a person more tolerant of evil. Think of a time in your life when you grew more tolerant of a negative thing over time. Describe the process of your growing tolerance. Why did you become less offended by the negative thing as time passed?
5. Answer the questions on p. 157: Who are the protagonists in your life? What outside influences affect your thinking, and, therefore, your desires? Are you in relationship with God in name only, or do you spend so much time with Him that He's the leading character in the story of your life?
6. Read and annotate 2 Corinthians 10 (using the Logic Of if necessary).
    - Golden Rule: every underline/highlight needs a corresponding comment

Epilogue

What's In A Name?

We started this book by talking about the names that people who didn't understand John the Baptist probably called him: lunatic, drunkard, crazy. And once they experienced his ministry, they saw him differently.

Why didn't those people steer John from his mission? We've seen how devastating character assassination can be to a person since we live in Cancel Culture. What someone calls you can have an immense impact on your life, so why wasn't John derailed?

John *heard* what people called him, but he more importantly *knew* what God called him. When we are in relationship with God and we know what He calls us, not even the worst mischaracterization or slander or untruths coming from others can take us off course.

We don't want your journey to stop here. Don't take this book as an authority on God and say that you know God more now because of what you've read in these pages. *Become* the authority on God by spending time with Him. Live by the name God calls you as you grow in a relationship with Him.

Our Hope

We believe that reading the Bible for yourself is a vital, continual process for any Christian. We recognize, however, that the Bible *seems* to contradict itself in many places. Consider the following example.

In Romans 14, Paul says that we should either do or refrain from doing things when we're around less mature believers based on their beliefs and understanding so as not to be a stumbling block to them. Romans 14:21 (NIV) says, "It is better not to eat meat or drink wine or to do anything else that will cause your brother or sister to fall." The message here seems clear: Consider how your actions affect your brothers and sisters in Christ, and refrain from doing things that will cause them to stumble in their faith.

But in 1 Corinthians 10, Paul seems to make the opposite point. Verses 25 and 26 (NIV) of that chapter say, "Eat anything sold in the meat market without raising questions of conscience, for, 'The earth is the Lord's, and everything in it.'" A little further down, in verse 29 (NIV), he says, "I am referring to the other person's conscience, not yours. For why is my freedom being judged by another's conscience?" It seems the takeaway from 1 Corinthians 10 is the opposite of the takeaway from Romans 14: eat whatever you want because it doesn't matter. On the surface, it seems like the Bible is in direct conflict with itself. But in order to fully understand the meaning of both texts, we must zoom out and look at the larger backdrop.

In both cases, Paul's point is not about food and drink, but about *relationships*. In Romans 14, Paul is talking about interacting with other members of the faith community. In 1 Corinthians 10, Paul is talking about relating to an unbeliever. In neither case is his point about the law; in both cases, his point is about the relationship.

Epilogue

Relationship is always God's priority because God is a person. God wants to spend eternity with us in an intimate, unbroken, loving relationship. This is the essence of Heaven, and this is why Heaven can begin right now. It is not an exaggeration to say that God will save everyone who will be happy in Heaven. In our spiritual journeys, we must ask ourselves if we're becoming the kinds of people who will be happy spending eternity with God *the person* and not just the *things* that come along with that. If what we're most looking forward to in Heaven is streets of gold and a mansion, then we're more interested in God's blessings for us than we are in God *Himself*. It's important that we evaluate our priorities so that we're focusing on the person rather than the product.

We have to make it a point to contextualize everything we do within the framework of love. If God is anything He's love first, and everything He is and does comes from His love. All expressions of His character are expressed through His love.

Admittedly, God's love is difficult to understand because we are inherently egocentric and sociocentric people. One of the downfalls (and benefits) of living in Western society is being able to control quite a bit of our own lives. When we have this freedom, it often leads to protecting ourselves (egocentric) and our own groups (sociocentric), but sometimes at the neglect of others outside of ourselves or our groups.

It should be our goal, always, to live in God's love and to express God's love. All other expressions of love (e.g., returning tithe, keeping our minds and bodies healthy, seeking God's Truth, etc.) can easily transform into expressions of hate when they are not intentionally and explicitly expressed through love. For example, seeking God's Truth can turn into hatred and mistreatment toward people who don't have the same Truth we profess *if* our search is not firmly planted in God's love. Returning tithe can very easily turn into a financial burden when we tithe out of obligation or a religious rule rather than as an expression of our love toward God. In short, without God's love, the line between good and evil is impossible to detect.

Within the context of religion, we often put a good thing in place of the best thing. For example, some religions may prioritize one particular rule that they firmly believe to the point where that rule is what they lead with. You ask them, "What does it mean to be [whatever denomination you are]," and their answer is, "We follow this particular rule." When that happens, the rule becomes a barrier between us and God when in fact, Jesus came to Earth to *remove* all barriers between us and God. We have a tendency, though, to focus more heavily on the law, or religious rules, which de-emphasizes the sacrifice that Jesus made for all of us.

We are not saying rules and boundaries aren't important, but we are saying that they aren't *more important* than our relationship with God and, therefore, our relationship with others. When we place rules too high on our list of priorities, we make it almost impossible to have loving relationships with one another and with God. God isn't bound by anything, including the law *which He created*.

To return to our vehicle analogy that we discussed in the introduction, each vehicle (religion) has different features (rules) that are specific to that vehicle. And we don't think there's anything wrong with that, unless the focus is more on the features than it is on the Driver, God.

Epilogue

The Gospel, the Good News, is that God has made peace with humanity through the sacrifice of Jesus Christ, and as a result of that sacrifice, every single person on Earth can be saved if they are willing to accept the gift of salvation that Jesus has purchased on our behalf. We run into problems, though, when we behave as though "The Gospel" only means keeping our favorite rule. The law is important, but keeping the law is the *effect* of having surrendered to God; it is not the *cause* of anyone's salvation. In fact, as the book of Romans attests, the law can only be fulfilled if it is expressed through the love of God.[1]

We encourage you to remain spiritually curious, to continue to seek truth in God as it is revealed in the Bible and in your walk with Him, and to live by the name God calls you. We hope the practical strategies we have given you in this book bear fruit in your relationship with God, but if they do not, we encourage you to come up with your own practical strategies for living a life with God, or to get together with Godly friends to try new things that will help you to develop your relationship with God. God will reward our efforts to sincerely seek Him so that we can know Him better.[2] We believe that what God wants the most is for us to want from Him what He wants from us—a close, loving relationship in which we discover what kind of person God really is.

---

[1] Romans 3:22; 4:14-16; 8:1-4; 13:8-10
[2] Matthew 7:7 (NIV): "Ask and it will be given to you; seek and you will find; knock and the door will be opened to you."

Comprehension Questions Based on the Chapter

1. What is the rhetorical situation (communicator, audience, and message) of the chapter, and why does this context matter?
2. What is the stated or implied thesis statement of the chapter?
3. What two biblical passages do the authors use to clear up the misguided view that the Bible contradicts itself?
4. How do the authors explain that Heaven can be experienced right now on Earth?
5. Why do the authors say putting "a good thing in place of the best thing" (p. 169) can be spiritually dangerous?

Writing Questions

1. Compare and contrast the message of Romans 14 with the message of 1 Corinthians 10. Some may think this is a case of the Bible contradicting itself. Explain why this is not a contradiction.
2. Evaluate your priorities. When it comes to spending time with God, what are your motivations? Why do you pray, or study the Bible, or go to church? If you don't do any of these things, why don't you? What spiritual activities do you engage in and why?
3. What is "The Gospel" and how does understanding what The Gospel is affect the way a Christian should live their life?

Epilogue

4. Why is it so common for religious people to emphasize the law over personal relationships? Write out 1 or 2 practical solutions to this problem.
5. Read and annotate 1 Corinthians 10 **or** Romans 14 (using the Logic Of if necessary). Golden Rule: every underline/highlight needs a corresponding comment.

CRITICAL THINKING ACTIVITIES

1. Complete a "Logic Of" the chapter [annotations & analysis] (see *The Miniature Guide to Critical Thinking* for a Logic of template and *The Thinker's Guide to Analytic Thinking* for Logic of examples)
   - Label/highlight the elements of thought throughout the chapter
   - Add a comment under each label explaining *why* you think that section is the element of thought (these are your annotations)
   - Use the elements of thought that you've identified to help you analyze the text
2. Write an SEE-I paragraph on a key concept in the chapter(see *How to Read a Paragraph*)
3. Paragraph paraphrase (see *How to Write a Paragraph*)
   - Choose 1 paragraph and write a paraphrase on that paragraph
4. Peer teaching activity (see *How to Read a Paragraph*)
   - Work with 1 classmate or friend; decide who is Person A and who is Person B
   - As a pair, focus on 1 section of the chapter you just read

- **Working separately**, Person A should read the first half of the section and take notes on it, and Person B should read the second half of the section and take notes on it
- **Working together,** Person A should teach Person B what they learned from the reading; Person B should practice focused listening
- **Working together,** when Person A is finished, Person B paraphrases what Person A taught
- **Working together,** switch roles and do it again (Person B teaches, Person A listens and paraphrases)
5. Use the Universal Intellectual Standards to assess any of the above activities (see *The Miniature Guide to Critical Thinking*)

All critical thinking activities are adapted from materials from The Foundation for Critical Thinking. For additional activities, refer to *How to Read a Paragraph* and *How to Write a Paragraph*.

STYLE QUESTIONS

1. What introduction strategy do the authors use? What concluding strategy do the authors use? How do the strategies affect how you engage with the chapter?
2. How do the authors use transitions throughout the chapter? How do the transition choices affect how you engage with the chapter?
3. How do the authors mix writing modes (e.g. narrative, argumentative, etc.) in the chapter? How do the writing modes affect how you engage with the chapter?
4. How do the authors integrate outside sources into their own writing?
5. Is the authors' word choice general and abstract or specific and concrete? How does the authors' diction affect how you engage with the chapter?
6. What parts of the chapter use a professional tone? What parts of the chapter use a conversational tone? How does the authors' tone affect how you engage with the chapter?

HELPFUL RESOURCES

Elder, Linda and Richard Paul. *The Thinker's Guide to The Human Mind* 4th ed. Foundation for Critical Thinking Press, 2015.

"College and University Students." *College and University Students*, https://www.criticalthinking.org/pages/college-and-university-students/799.

Critical Thinking, https://www.criticalthinking.org/store/catalogs/thinkers-guides/224.

Lunsford, Andrea A. *The Everyday Writer with Exercises* 6th ed. Bedford / St. Martin's, 2016.

Nixon, Paul D. and Clarise Nixon. *God Is A Person: Discovering God For Yourself*. True Vine Publishing, 2021.

Nosich, Gerald. *Critical Writing: A Guide to Writing a Paper Using the Concepts and Processes of Critical Thinking*. Rowman & Littlefield, 2022.

Paul, Richard and Linda Elder. *Critical Thinking: Tools for Taking Charge of Your Learning and Your Life* 4th ed. Rowman & Littlefield, 2021.

—. *How to Read a Paragraph: The Art of Close Reading* 2nd ed. Rowman & Littlefield.

—. *How to Write a Paragraph: The Art of Substantive Writing* 3rd ed. Rowman & Littlefield.

—. *The Miniature Guide to Critical Thinking Concepts & Tools* 8th ed. Rowman & Littlefield.

www.ingramcontent.com/pod-product-compliance
Lightning Source LLC
LaVergne TN
LVHW010259260326
834688LV00044B/1370